MOUNTAINS OF MOAB

THE DIARY OF A YEOMAN
1908 – 1919

Including Gallipoli and Palestine
during the Great War
E .V. GODRICH

EDITED AND PUBLISHED BY HIS SON
DR. JOHN GODRICH

First edition 2011

Printed in China

A catalogue record for this book is available from the
British Library

ISBN 978 0 954 904 395

ACCREDITATIONS

To my friend Masoud Akhbari, whose inspiration and experience with publishing has encouraged me to produce this version of my father's memoirs. He has edited, arranged and produced the text in its present form. He has co-operated with the printers in China to produce this beautiful edition and advised me regarding its distribution. Masoud is author of "*The Dutch amongst the Persians 1696-1979*"

To Mrs. Olive Day who has transposed and corrected the text from a Remington typed version with addenda onto computer disc ready for minor editing and publication.

To Col. Stamford Cartwright, Chairman of Committee of the Queens Own Worcestershire Hussars Museum Trustees for their constant support and encouragement and their help in making available material and literature in their care and help with distribution.

To the Warwickshire and Worcestershire Yeomanry Combined Trust for information and photographs and help with distribution, and the curators of the Regimental museums at Warwick and Worcester.

To the Imperial War Museum for copies of their archives and photographs included in the diary.

To the late Colonel Lord Hampton for his gift to the Q.O.W.H of the watercolours painted in the desert while in command of the regiment, published for the first time in this diary.

To my friend Major Paul Fowler Smith for contributing the photographs from his collection of militaria and uniforms of the Yeomanry.

To the officers and committee of the Gallipoli Association, in particular to Col. Michael Hickey and Maj. Hugh Jenner for their advice and encouragement.

To my nephew Mr. Robin Norton for gathering information on the Regimental history, shipping, participation of the Anzacs and French Armies at Gallipoli and thanks for accompanying me on a trip to Gallipoli in 2006 to visit the battlefields.

To my daughter Zara for help with transferring data records and her husband Richard Humphry for transferring the photos from my fathers diary. Also Charles Woolmer, Alan Jones and Pamela Wood for help with computer problems.

Foreword

by

Major Sir Jerry Wiggin T.D.

It is a sad fact that most people in this Country are unaware that the First World War was fought anywhere else but France and against any other enemy except the Germans. It is therefore very welcome that Dr. John Godrich has gone to a great deal of trouble to collect together his Father's papers - mostly his diary and publish them with some other relevant documents including Lord Hampton's watercolour drawings which tell the story of the large volunteer Army that defended the Suez Canal and Railway against the Turkish invasion that was intended to cut off this vital link for Britain to India and the Far East.

Victor Godrich was born in 1887 some nine months before my own Father. He was educated at the best Grammar School in Birmingham (later on my Father was a Governor) and joined the Queen's Own Worcestershire Hussars (The Worcestershire Yeomanry) at about the same time. The Haldane Reforms at that time included the formation of the Territorial Army in the wake of the Boer War and were in place to harness the will of thousands of loyal volunteers to serve their Country in a professional and gallant manner.

This book is both unusual and valuable because unlike most Histories it is not written as a record of the movement of Armies or as an Officer's diary but from the viewpoint of an ordinary soldier. Well educated he has written a fascinating and readable account of the many discomforts of life from the disaster of Gallipoli to the victorious capture of Damascus. He has every Tommy's view of his officers and describes without too much complaint the appalling suffering of men and horses as they harried the Turk up and down the desert. Heat, thirst, hunger and sickness were every man's lot and owing to distances relief was infrequent. When medical assistance was available it was primitive by modern standards and all ranks suffered in the extremes of heat and cold in this region of desert and the land of milk and honey. The enemy was cunning and energetic and well led by their Prussian Generals. Their supply lines were overland and well in place by the time the defenders arrived to challenge them.

The arrival of General Allenby turned the battle but put an even greater burden on the Cavalry who responded magnificently leading to ultimate victory. The close contact with the enemy led to many casualties, brave deeds and severe fatigue to men and horses.
This book should be compulsory reading for any student of the Palestine Campaign from 1914 to 1919. This was the last Campaign in history fought mainly with horses that was brought to a successful conclusion.

My Father died when I was just fifteen and too young to hear his account of much that went on but he must have known Victor Godrich well. In the Second World War he commanded the Worcestershire Home Guard and one of his Officers was Col. Godrich who commanded the Post Office Section. What wonderful men they were.
MEMBERS OF THE WIGGIN FAMILY ASSOCIATED WITH THE Q.O.W.H. DURING THE PALESTINIAN CAMPAIGN

Brigadier-General Edgar A.Wiggin D.S.O.,D.L. J.P. (1867-1939) 13th Hussars. Wounded Chocolate Hill Gallipoli 18.9.15. Commanded 1st Mounted Brigade in Gallipoli and Sinai. Buried at Newbold Pacey.

Colonel W.Walter Wiggin Commissioned 1891 Commanded 2/1 Worcestershire Yeomanry 1915-1916.

Colonel Sir William (Bill) Wiggin D.S.O., T.D., D.L.,J.P.
Nephew of W.W.W. Commissioned 1907.
Commanded 'C' Squadron Apr. 1915. Gallipoli, Egypt and Palestine. Mentioned in dispatches 5 times.
Wounded at Katia. Led the Worcester squadron in the charge at Huj Nov.1917. Bar to D.S.O.
Jan.1918 O/C Sherwood Rangers. March 1939 Colonel of 53rd Anti-tank Regt Royal Artillery.
Hon Col. of Q.O.W.H. 1948-51. Chairman Worcs. Territorial Assocn 1936-56.

Captain G.R. Wiggin (Bob) son of WWW Commissioned 1907
Embarked for Egypt Apr 1915. Killed on Easter Sunday at Oghratina, Sinai.

PREFACE

Colonel (H/G) Edward Victor Godrich, Queens Own Worcestershire Hussars. He was born at Henley in Arden Warwickshire on 5th May 1887. He was the son of a grocer, who ran the grocery store near the old Parish Church where he lived with his parents and sisters Winnie Evelyn and Gladys. His brother Norman died in infancy of Pneumonia. Victor went to King Edwards Grammar School in Birmingham and captained the rugby football team. He was taken on by the G.P.O. at the age of 17 as an employee, ten years before the war.

At this time the Territorial Army was being enlarged and reformed; the wealthy nations of Europe were becoming militant in their attitudes to one another. Although Queen Victoria was the Queen with an Empire on which the sun never set, and had members of her family seated on several thrones of Europe, including Kaiser William of Germany, the nations vied with one another to be the most powerful. Heavy armaments and enormous navies were produced and the size of the Armed forces increased rapidly, ostensibly to protect and control their new colonies.

Although he was living in Warwickshire he enrolled in the Worcestershire Yeomanry in 1908. He hired a horse for annual camp and drilled regularly at weekends with the growing Regiment.

The Earl of Dudley, when he was Colonel of the Regiment, paid for each man to be issued with a steel sword and scabbard made by Wilkinson's. The Army provided the serge uniform and peaked hat. The officers usually owned their own horses which they used for hunting and the O.R.s hired or borrowed mounts on which to practise drill or attend camp.

 It was not long before War with Germany was declared in 1914. The unpopular Archduke Ferdinand of Austria on an unwise visit to Sarajevo was assassinated by a Serbian nationalist. The large power block of Austro-Hungary was destabilised and the European nations, including Turkey and Russia took sides in the scramble to secure additional territory and people.

Upon declaration of War, apart from the Regular soldiers and sailors mobilisation involved only volunteers. The famous poster of Kitchener, C-in-C, pointing at the onlooker demanding YOU to volunteer resulted in sufficient numbers, at least until the killing began.

The Worcestershire Yeomanry being a T.A. Regiment was at first an entirely voluntary Organisation and it was one of the first to be shipped abroad to the Middle East. The Turks of the Ottoman Empire with military advisers from Germany threatened to capture the Suez Canal. The Cavalry Brigade also contained the Warwickshire and Gloucestershire Yeomanry Regiments, all T.A. with some Regular Army officers. Cavalry were ill suited to the trench warfare in Belgium and France, but very useful in the mobile tactics of the battles in the Sinai Desert and Palestine.

Thousands of horses were compulsorily purchased from the Shires; draught horses for pulling heavy guns and hunters and hacks for the mounted troops. Steam engines, caterpillar tractors and petrol engines were shipped abroad only later in the game.

The battles and everyday activity from Gaza to Damascus are related on a week by week basis in this personal and easily read diary, which he kept up throughout the war. As an expert machine gunner he was directed to Gallipoli on the Suvla Bay landing and after a few weeks of trench On demobilisation in 1919 he was fortunate to be taken on again by the Post Office

He married Dorothy Faithfull of Studley, Warwickshire, a farmer's daughter, educated at a French convent in Dieppe, she was housekeeper to her uncle Job Penzer, a local J.P. and tax- collector, who lived on a small farmstead in Barnt Green. Victor lived there for fifty years and helped her to transform it into a beautiful house with garden, tennis court, paddock and orchard.

By 1930 they had three children, Yvonne Mary, Dorothy Anne, and John Edward. Victor was a Special Constable in the turbulent twenties, treasurer and later Chairman of the Barnt Green British Legion, which won two trophies for their fund raising. He was awarded the Legion's Gold medal.

He was a local Parish councillor, Chairman of Bromsgrove RDC and a Worcester County Councillor.
He chaired the Horticultural society which held a memorable flower show at his home The Poplars every year. In 1939 at the outbreak of the Second World War, he was working in the survey department of the GPO establishing and building regional head post offices in the suburbs of Birmingham.

Introduction

He was one of the first to join the Home Guard, and due to his wartime experience, his clerical organising ability and local knowledge he was made Colonel, Midland Zone Commander for the Post Office Home Guard.

He was undoubtedly a survivor, full of good humour, always ready to help anyone who suffered, and devoted to a life of public service. He was able to befriend both rich and poor, and never tolerated unfair behaviour.

After the death of his wife Dorothy, the Poplars estate was sold and he went to live with his sister Gladys in Hazlemere Surrey.
He died on April 4th 1981 and his ashes are interred alongside Dorothy who is buried in Cofton Hackett graveyard in Barnt Green Parish Worcestershire.

EVG. Kings Lynn. April 1915.

Corporal Edward Victor Godrich
Queens Own Worcestershire Hussars

Colonel Edward Victor GODRICH b.5.5.1887.

WORCESTERSHIRE YEOMANRY 1914-19 1908-19 Special 1921-9 Defence Medal 1940-45
1914 Star British War Victory Medal Territorial Force Constabulary WWII
Medal Efficiency Medal long service Zone Commander
Egypt Gallipoli Palestine Syria Midland Home Guard

When you read this book, think always of the horses who took part
in the war. They were shipped by the thousand to take part in the
campaign; heavy beasts for pulling carts and stores behind the lines
and quicker lighter horses for carrying communications and
soldiers about their business. A cavalry regiment had up to 400
horses in action at full strength, and 300 in use every day with
blacksmith farriers and grooms and veterinary surgeons to tend
them.

The most famous event in the history of the Worcestershire
Yeomanry is the cavalry charge at Huj, when two troops of men
from the Regiment led by Major Bill Wiggin and Captain
Valentine combined with two troops of the Warwickshire
Regiment to charge for 1500 yards into the face of the Austrian
field guns. This was as brave an action as the famous charge of the
Light Brigade in the Crimean War, and is reputed to be the last
known charge against field guns in our History. My father was not
allowed to take part, so was probably spared his life, but he
witnessed it and had the unpleasant task with others in burying the
dead and disposing of the injured horses. (see Nov.8th 1917).

It is difficult to trace what happened to the horses after the war was
ended. Some of the officers managed to ship their beloved hunters
back to England, but although Lord Hampton brought many back
from Damascus in his march home in 1919 to Alexandria the
majority of war horses were sold to dealers and then used by Arab
merchants with carts.

When Lady Alan Brooke went to Cairo a few years later she discovered in Cairo many horses marked with the War Department arrow on their rump being abused, emaciated and diseased. She founded the Brooke Hospital in Cairo by raising thousands of Pounds in Britain, and this Charity now called The Brooke is expanding its activity throughout the Middle East. It gives advice to the inhabitants, treats the animals and sometimes purchases them from bad owners to give them some respite and a painless end.

The drama War Horse is playing to full houses in London as this goes to press; it tells the story of a horse and its owner who go to the battlefields of France. Imagine them in the dusty grassless waterless sun-stricken desert of Palestine.

J.E.G. 1.7.11.

CONTENTS

Acknowledgements Pg 2

Foreword Pg 3

Preface Pg 5

Introduction Pg 7

Map of Palestine Pg 13 and in Appendix 8.

Mountains of Moab Pg 14

War Diary

Chapter 1 Introduction to a War Story Pg 15

Chapter 2 Preparing for War with the Territorial Army Pg 18

Chapter 3 What did YOU do in the Great War Daddy? Pg 22

Chapter 4 Overseas on Active Service (1915) Pg 35

Chapter 5 Arrival in Egypt Pg 37

Chapter 6 City of Cairo Pg 40

Chapter 7 The Citadel (1915) Pg 46

Chapter 8 Embarkation for Gallipoli Pg 50

Chapter 9 Gallipoli Landing at Suvla Bay Pg 52

Chapter 10 Baptism of Fire (21st of August 1915) Pg 56

Chapter 11 Farewell to Gallipoli (1915) Pg 69

Chapter 12 Homeward Bound. Recovery from Typhoid (January
          1916) at Whalley Hospital Pg 72

Chapter 13 My Second Trip out East Pg 75

Chapter 14 On Board the Liner Kalyan from Marseille Pg 79

Chapter 15 Return to Sinai Desert Pg 81

Chapter 16 Rafa 100 Miles North of Suez Pg 83

 Chapter 17 First Battle of Gaza (26th March 1917) Pg 90

Chapter 18 Midnight Raid Pg 93

Chapter 19 Second Battle of Gaza Pg 101

Chapter 20 General Allenby Takes Command Pg 107

Chapter 21 Lord Hampton O/C "D" Squadron. Confirmation by
          the Bishop of Jerusalem Pg 110

Chapter 22 Battle of Beersheba Pg 115

Chapter 23 Huj: the Glorious Charge Pg 122

Chapter 24 Christmas in the Mountains Pg 142

Chapter 25 Back in the Valley Pg 145

Chapter 26 Amwas Pg 153

Chapter 27 Cavalry Raid on Es Salt, Trans-Jordan Pg 154

Chapter 28 Jericho and Ramallah Pg 159

Chapter 29 Sickness: Sent to Kantara for recovery Pg 168

Chapter 30 'Holiday'! Horse Racing and Parades Pg 175

Chapter 31 Cana in Galilee and Nazareth Pg 179

Chapter 32 Mount Hermon Pg 181

Chapter 33   Damascus Pg 184
Chapter 34   Armistice 30th of October 1918 Pg 188
Chapter 35 Peace at Last   Pg 190
Chapter 36 Journey Home Pg 193

APPENDICES

Appendix 1 Watercolours Painted by Lord Hampton Pg 197
Appendix 2 Militaria Collection of Major P. Fowler-Smith Pg 214
Appendix 3 Allied Cemetery at Lone Pine, Gallipoli Pg 218
Appendix 4 Suvla Bay Poem by W.H.Littlejohn Pg 219
Appendix 5 Verses and Poems and Epilogue Pg 220
    1) "Q.O.W.H" Poem by Oscar Teichmann (Regimental MO)
    2) Relieving Guard by Bret Harte Pg 223
Appendix 6 Letter to Victor Godrich about Katia Pg 228
Appendix 7 Major Ffrench Blake Pg 230
Appendix 8 Additional Photographs Pg 233
    Anglican Archbishop of Jerusalem Pg 238

13

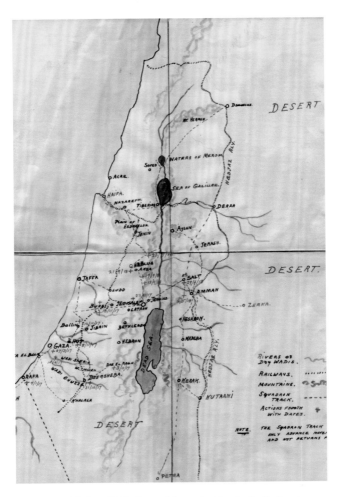

Map of Syria and Palestine and the routes taken by the Regiment

MOUNTAINS OF MOAB

One of the most captivating views in the world is that from the top of the Mount of Olives, looking over the River Jordan to the mountains of Moab beyond. It is a panorama of unique splendour and a scene of ever-changing lights, from a deep hazy blue to a rich rosy pink, and the colouring is never the same for five consecutive minutes. The more you look on the mountains of Moab the more you feel that behind them lie interest and romance; beyond this barrier lies the country of Transjordania, a land of great natural charm and one full of antiquities of immense interest.

The road from Jerusalem to Jericho drops 2000 feet then crosses the river Jordan in the Plain of Moab, at the Allenby bridge. Here the scene changes; the semi-civilised country of Palestine is left behind and the Bedouin country begins. The Eastern side of the Jordan is covered with dense thickets, and beyond, the mounds and hills are a barren glaring white. In summer the land is barren, but in springtime it is covered with beautiful wild flowers. This road to Damascus is where Saint Paul was converted to spread the Gospel of Christianity. It is precipitous and in many places it is hewn out of the rock, winding through valleys thick with blue flowering oleander bushes and watered by trickling streams and springs until on passing round a sharp corner the ancient town of Es Salt is revealed. Here the advance of Victor Godrich's cavalry brigade was halted by the Turkish riflemen and snipers. They had to leave their horses behind under cover and act like infantrymen. He nearly lost his life in going to rescue an injured comrade under fire and the Regiment had to retire down the valley after many casualties. Not for six months was Es Salt taken and the advance to Damascus achieved by a massive force of Anzac infantry and Light Horse Regiments.

This is just one place where Victor nearly lost his life. Read on and discover his braveness and his frailty, a great survivor who lived to write his tale.

J.E.G.

Chapter 1

Introduction to a War Story

This war diary was compiled by E. Victor Godrich of the Queen's Own Worcestershire Hussars (QOWH)

The Regiment of Worcestershire Yeomanry was formed in 1794 to protect the country from a threatened invasion from France, but after Waterloo (1815) the threat disappeared and the Regiment (Regt.) was disbanded.

Civil disorders were common so the Regiment was revived in 1830. From then the Regiment was maintained and kept alive by the gentlemen and landowners of the country.

The title of Queen's Own was conferred on the Regiment by Queen Victoria in recognition of the protection of Her Majesty during her visit to Hewell Grange in 1832.

01- The Yeomen

The war against the Boers changed everything because the Army that was sent to South Africa was chiefly Infantry. The Boers were mainly farmers mounted on horses. The War Office realised that mounted Infantry were required. All Yeomanry regiments were invited to call for volunteers for service abroad. A squadron of 120 men was selected from Worcestershire. They formed part of the **5th Regiment of Imperial Yeomanry** and served abroad until peace was declared in 1902.

The experience gained in the Boer War demonstrated to the War Office that Yeomanry, used as Mounted Infantry, could be effective. New khaki uniforms were issued for drills and camps.

Following this improvement, the government of the day introduced a Bill in 1907 which created a new Army named *"The Territorials"*. This combined all branches of activity into Divisions. The Act was passed and volunteers called for. The response was remarkable and many regiments were recruited up to strength. In November 1908, when I was 21 years old, together with several others I decided to join a Yeomanry Regiment.

The nearest we could find was the Worcestershire Yeomanry who had a squadron headquarters at Kings Heath where we were inspected and tested by a Critical Officer and a Sergeant Major.

If approved, we were taken to a local JP where we swore loyalty to the King and Regiment.

Ability to ride a horse was not necessary, but there were several Orders that we had to obey: 3 Drills on foot and one mounted during the year.

The Yeomen in the above photograph are thought to be the Bromsgrove Troop (about 1905) in their khaki uniforms and Bush hats. Note the awkward position of their rifles.

The only one who can be identified is the man on the pony on the extreme right. This is John Field of Bromsgrove. His son, Signaller G H Field, served with us in Palestine. He took part in the Charge at Huj armed only with his signalling flags!

02- With the lads camping. Note the hobbled rear leg

The most important Order was attendance at Annual Camp for 14 days, this requirement created problems for those of us who were employed by firms not in sympathy with the New Army.

To those of us who were junior clerks or postmen, GPO Headquarters gave a ruling that Drills must be attended in our own time, absence at Camps was sanctioned but wages for one week only would be paid. Further time of absence would be deducted from our annual holiday.

There was some murmuring at this decision but we were volunteers keen to become Cavalrymen. The decision made in 1909 was maintained until August 1914. The First Camp as a TA regiment was held at Hanley Castle near Upton on Severn in 1908, but the regiment was not at full strength or efficiency.

My first appearance in uniform was at the burial of Lord Windsor, eldest son and heir to the Earl of Plymouth.

The Earl had commanded the regiment for many years and his son was a Lieutenant. After firing a salute over the grave, we marched to Hewell Grange where we were entertained to lunch. I thought this was an excellent start to my Army service.

A few months later, in May, we were summoned to report to Squadron Headquarters. My Squadron 'B', mostly Birmingham men, was conveyed to Worcester where we joined the rest of the regiment and were taken to Tidworth, Hants.

A few miles away we found a large camp prepared with tents and horse lines. The camp was for the whole Brigade, Warwick's, Gloucester's and Worcester's along with RAMC, RASC etc. **Perham Down** was some miles from the nearest habitation, so our only relaxation in the evening was the regimental canteen.

The weather was wet and stormy, the discipline strict, but we had several Field Days with sham fights that were interesting and enjoyable on the wide open space of Salisbury Plain.

At the last day in camp we were honoured by a visit paid by **Lieutenant General Sir Ian Hamilton** under whom we were destined to serve six years later. Perham Down was an excellent introduction for Officers and other ranks to Army life in the TA.

Windmill Hill 1910: We had a similar annual training camp on the 'Plain'. I have a note telling me that the regiment was supplied with short Lee-Enfield rifles and a second Maxim gun.

The latter were obviously relics from the South African War. We used them five years later on Gallipoli.

Chapter 2

PREPARING FOR WAR WITH THE TERRITORIAL ARMY

Training at Camp Elmley Castle 1911

03- Elmley Castle camp, Bredon Hill in background E.V.Godrich on saddle

03a - Sergeant Major Viner, well groomed and polished

03b – Major John Cartland. His son Ronald and his brother lost their lives on consecutive days during the retreat to Dunkirk in WW2 while serving with QOWH

O.4 Worcestershire Territorial Yeomanry Camp at Elmley Castle 1911

05 - (Left – right)   Godrich, Skudder, Ireland, Deakin

07 –The Regimental CSM   Newbury Camp

1911

We had a Regimental Camp at **Elmley Castle** at the foot of Bredon Hill in beautiful weather – an easy camp.

1912

Another Regimental Camp, at Eastnor Park, Malvern. A very wet camp. We had to move the horses every few days out of the muddy standings they created. In spite of the bad weather, a record of 439 (all Ranks) attended.

1913

Another Brigade Camp was on Salisbury Plain, this time at **Bulford,** as before, all three regiments and auxiliaries. By this time Officers and men were becoming well trained in Army life and we were amused at mixing with regular Army units who were in **Tidworth Barracks**. One day we had a sham battle with the regulars, we were soon defeated and captured because they knew every yard of the Plain and we did not.

It was a very useful experience for us. Sad to relate, Bulford was the last training camp we had. There were other items of interest during 1913:

- (a) Lieutenant Colonel Sir F Grey resigned and Lieutenant Colonel The Earl of Dudley took command of the regiment.
- (b) Captain Leslie Cheape of the Dragoon Guards was appointed Adjutant.

Lieutenant Colonel the Earl of Dudley had some experience in the regular Army having been attached to several Cavalry regiments, in order to fit himself for the command of our regiment. The most important alteration he made was to equip the whole regiment with the new Wilkinson Thrusting Swords and riding whips.

This changed the character of the regiment from Mounted Infantry to Cavalry, in line with the regular Cavalry. I believe we were the first Yeomanry Regiment to be so armed.

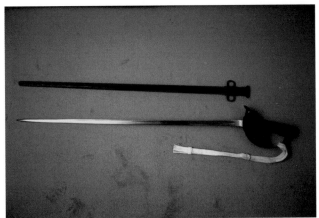

Another novelty our new C.O. made was to buy out a dozen regulars, experienced men to stiffen up us amateurs. Both the above measures were carried out at the expense of our C.O.

THE START OF THE GREAT WAR (1914)

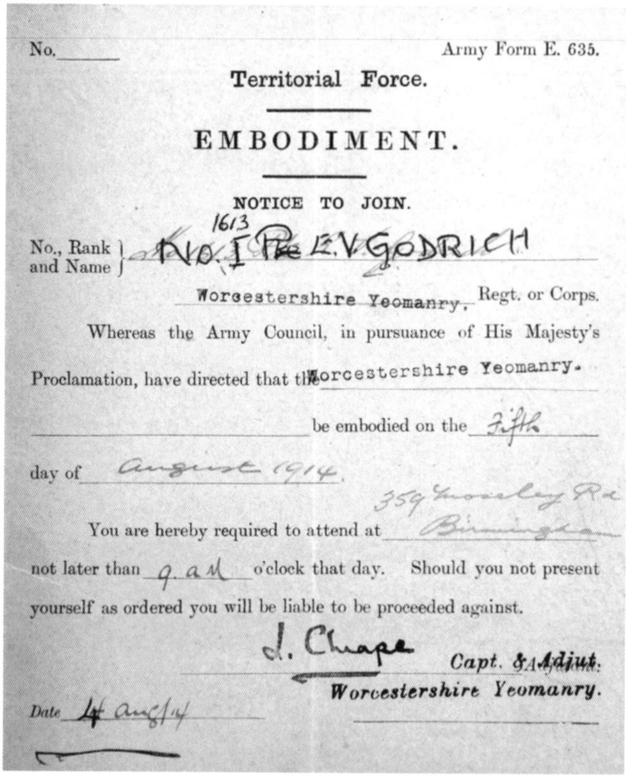

No._____   Army Form E. 635.

Territorial Force.

EMBODIMENT.

NOTICE TO JOIN.

No., Rank } *1613* No. I Pte. E. V. GODRICH
and Name }

_____Woroestershire Yeomanry._ Regt. or Corps.

Whereas the Army Council, in pursuance of His Majesty's

Proclamation, have directed that the Worcestershire Yeomanry.

_____ be embodied on the *Fifth*

day of *August 1914*.

359 Moseley Rd

You are hereby required to attend at _____ *Birmingham*

not later than _*9 a.m.*_ o'clock that day. Should you not present

yourself as ordered you will be liable to be proceeded against.

J. Chape *Capt. & Adjut.*
                                    Worcestershire Yeomanry.

Date *4 aug/14*

Two days after the declaration of war on Germany this notice of
embodiment was delivered to number 1613 Private E.V.Godrich.
By the time of his enlistment for National service on 17th Nov.
1949, his son John was issued with the number 22310505, over
twenty-two million more.

Daddy, what did *YOU* do in the Great War?

Chapter 3

What Did You Do In The Great War Daddy?

It has struck me that with luck; I might one day be asked the above rather awkward question by a son or daughter seeking the truth.

So I have recorded the episodes and journeys in which I took part before time blotted them from my memory.

This does not purport to be a War Novel, merely the plain recital of my experiences preceding and during the Great War. It will have one redeeming feature, it is the truth.

When War broke out I had been a member of the Worcestershire Yeomanry for nearly six years, having enlisted on 30th November 1908, so I had at least a nodding acquaintance with soldiering.

On 3rd August 1914: I was to be found on Sutton Park Rifle Range near Kidderminster, where the Regimental Musketry competitions were in progress.

It was a very enjoyable little camp. The weather was fine, the company good and altogether was a far better way of spending the weekend than mixing with the crowds at some seaside town.

The shooting for the Regimental Cup was fixed for Bank Holiday Monday, 4th August. I was proud to be shooting in my Squadron's team for the first time.

We were almost through with the shoot when a messenger came up with a telegram which he handed to the Adjutant, Captain Leslie Cheape.

There was a great deal of tension in the air, I recollect. We were all expecting something. Captain Cheape opened the telegram and read out to us that **War had been Declared**. We were to break up camp at once and hurry back to our homes.

What a waste of time everyone thought at once. Here we are in uniform with our rifles and ammunition, why not get across to France straight away, what else did we want? We had a lot to learn in those days. What excitement we all felt. What discussions we had with our threats to the German Army for daring to fight England.

How we crowded round old Sergeant Major Downes and plied him with questions. Did he think we would get a look-in at this little campaign that had just commenced, or would it all be over before we had our horses and equipment?

Jack was a wise old bird for he assured us that it would last much longer than we thought, undoubtedly we should be wanted.

We packed up and left Kidderminster that day. On the Tuesday I went to the office and put in a full day.

I am afraid that most of it was spent discussing the situation, already I was feeling proud to have a uniform to get into, which was much better than being a 'mere civilian'.

Tuesday night there was only one place to go. That of course was Squadron Headquarters where I found a very noisy, busy crowd.

Two or three were assisting Sergeant Major Osborne to send out 'mobilisation notices', the remainder were demanding buttons, pull-throughs and other important things at this critical time.

We received our notices on Wednesday morning **6th August 1914** warning us that we were called upon *"to present ourselves at*

Squadron Headquarters at 9.00 am and were under direct penalties should we fail to put in an appearance".

At 10.00 am we gathered to meet for the first time Major Hugh Gray-Cheape who had been posted to Command B Squadron. We drew everything that Sergeant Major Osborne had to issue.

At 2.00 pm we entrained at Camp Hill Station for Worcester, speeded by a large crowd of loving Mothers, Sisters and sweethearts.

I need hardly say that there were wet eyes in the crowd. The most brutal thing of all now took place. We were lined up on the platform and our Identification Discs were handed out. We had to tell the girls that they were given to us to wear in case we were blown to pieces, thus our corpses could be identified.

Well, wasn't it likely to be the finishing touch to a sad farewell!

08 - QOWH band photo taken in 1909 (the band disbanded in August 1914)

09 – Entraining horses, camp Hill

09A – Newbury Camp

10 - Cookhouse at Newbury September 1914

We spent a very happy week at Worcester, during which time the County was scoured for horses, the mounts allotted and passed for service. I was billeted at the Sandpits Inn, Bromyard Road together with Harry Scudder, T Baker and A Wood.

I have grateful memories of the way we were treated by Mr & Mrs Smith, not least by Elsie.

Whilst at Worcester, Austin Woodward, Tillyer, Shorthouse and I (4 B Squadron men) were informed that we were henceforth machine gunners under Lieutenant R J Watts. This had a big influence on my part in the War which I did not foresee in those happy days.

Being four Birmingham men pitch-forked into a crowd of Worcester fellows we did not know, we resented it and were determined to leave the Gun Section at the first opportunity. However, we soon were at home with the strangers and became pals. This eventually ripened into several friendships which remained delightful memories.

From Worcester we moved to **Warwick** where we met the Warwick's and Gloucester Yeomanry. We were now a Brigade. We only stayed four days which was quite enough as we were now in the throes of regimental cooking and the cooks were new to the work.

The food put before us was not very palatable, added to this was the fact that our mess rooms were in a school which was being repainted. You will understand why the restaurants in Warwick and Leamington did so well during our visit!

During this time, Tom Tillyer was thrown from his horse and sustained a fractured shoulder, he went to hospital and we did not see him again.

From Warwick we entrained for **Bury St. Edmunds**. The MG Section was dumped at Rushbrook Hall Farm, far from the madding crowd. We slept in good clean barns and had an ample supply of clean straw.

The farmer, Mr Brown, was a good old sort; a few of us had several merry singsongs in his house.

It was very hot and there was not much water on the farm, so we had no alternative but to journey to Bury St. Edmunds (approx. 3 miles) in the evenings to quench our thirsts.

Whilst at this farm we lost a horse during the night following "stand to your horses" about 6 times on a boiling hot day. Our incapable Officer at last discovered which horse it was.

This was not any use however, for although we found his number, we never found the horse! So he was "struck off strength". My diary says that the password here was "What's the number of your horse and are you quite clear?"

Whilst at Rushbrook we had our first alarm. Arriving back from Bury one evening about 11.00 pm we were immediately hustled off to Regimental Headquarters to draw ball ammunition.

We found RSM Morlidge distributing this nasty stuff to all within his reach. "I haven't a rifle Sir" was no excuse. It was like castor oil, you had to have it.

Back to our farms post-haste where we set to work by the light of feeble farm lamps to load guns, MG belts etc. into our transport ready for an immediate "Marching Order".

Our rapid transport at this stage was a quartet of real Cannock Chase coal carts. If only we had been at Mons with them, we should have astounded the German Army! I am certain however, they came in useful for other purposes than carrying MGs as I will presently show.

The excitement of our "Stand To" soon died down, to which we never discovered the reason. Some said that a German Landing was expected in Norfolk, others that Yarmouth had been bombarded.

Whatever it was we heard afterwards that 'A' Squadron had saddled up and stood in a field all night. We of the MGs never did silly things like that unless under the strictest compulsion, so we enjoyed a good night's sleep.

One of the many little services that our trusty coal carts performed was actually work of the kind that they had been built for. The cooks wanted coal – it had to be fetched from Bury.

Needham, Frank Davenall and Tysoe were the lucky transport drivers. I shall never forget their beautiful pearly teeth and shining eyes set in coal black faces that we beheld on their return.

They had loaded about 3 tons of coal with their hands and brought it up to Rushbrook.

I often thought of those fatigues years afterwards when 1917-18 recruits grumbled at having to do a 10 minute job.

After a week at the farm, we moved into the Park close by, under canvas. The Regiment was together for the first time. It was very hot; our rations were short, so much so that we scoured round the country for meals.

A small party of us found a cottage where we regularly had a square meal every night. The dear old lady was terribly apologetic at charging us 9d each – not much profit out of that!

At Rushbrook Park the Regiment indulged in a night march round the neighbouring country – to test our ability to keep together. The MGs and transport brought up the rear of the column and we went jogging along the dark lanes.

We soon discovered that coal wagons could not keep up with cavalry. When dawn broke we realised that we were lost.

Our much 'esteemed' Officer and the Transport Officer, Lieutenant Todd, tried gamely to hide the truth from us but it was too obvious. After a long detour we arrived back in camp four or five hours after the Regiment. We had an amusing Church Parade in this camp. The service was held near the horses. On the congregation opening their lungs for 'Fight the Good Fight' a lot of nags broke loose and went galloping about causing a lot of amusement to the boys and an abrupt end to the service!

At Rushbrook we were finally asked to volunteer for Foreign Service. The 'sheep' were divided from the 'goats'.

The non-volunteers were sent back to Worcester and were replaced by a fine lot of volunteer recruits who had joined up after the declaration of War.

We met the Oxford Yeomanry who went out to France as Infantry and took part in many battles in 1914.

It was here that I got into my first bit of trouble, being put under arrest for lending a Head Collar to a pal. Our silly Officer threatened me with a Court Martial which I avoided by a timely expression of regret.

The following day I was made a Full Corporal! I don't know if there was any connection or purely coincidence.

After a week we trekked to Norwich in two days, halting the first night in Redgrave Park near Botesdale, Suffolk (25 miles) and in a stubble field just outside Norwich the second night.

Reveille at 4.00 am, we entrained at 5.30 am then journeyed through London to **Newbury, Berkshire (30th August 1914)**. Here we had a fine camp on the famous race course – the whole Brigade now being complete with Artillery, RAMC, and ASC.

We had some amusement with the German civilians who were interned on the course behind barbed wire.

The Birmingham men were surprised to see amongst them the pre-war manager of the Colonnade Hotel.

11 – Machine Gun section in training at Worcester 16 Aug.1914

12 - Maxim Machine Gun section Worcestershire Hussars

A few days after our arrival we had a nasty stampede, some 500 horses breaking loose and galloping all over the country at about 10.00 pm on a dark night.

When morning came we found dead animals. Injuries were numerous. Some of the poor animals were found as far away as Hungerford (12 miles), most of them with scars and cuts.

We were now an overseas unit and training started in earnest. The MG Section received a new Sergeant (Pikey Adams) and several recruits (Goodson, Field, and Middleton, King, Smith, Hewins, Poole to name but a few).

Inoculation against enteric fever laid us low for a few days. We were issued with the new SLE Mark 2 Rifle, pointed ammo, swords and complete saddlery. We finally felt that we should not be pottering in England for much longer.

October 1914: We broke camp as the weather was getting bad and our horses were feeling the effect of this. We went into billets in Newbury, the MGs were sent to the pretty village of Newtown about 1½ miles out of town where we were the guests of Lady Arbuthnot (we used her barn).

We were at Newtown for approx. 3 weeks, it was a veritable holiday. Our Officer sprained his ankle and never came near us, while Sergeant Adams had his wife down at Newbury, so he was too busy to attend.

We did not progress much towards fully trained soldiers, but we had a really good time. Lady Arbuthnot, Reverend Grundy, Mr Willoughby and several gentlemen of the district did their best to make our stay a pleasant one – which it certainly was a beautiful bit of England.

I did learn one thing at Newtown which came in useful afterwards the game of 'Solo'. My tutor was my very best pal, Cyril Coombes.

It was at Newtown that Billy Hill joined the MG Section. Billy was very annoyed at being placed on driving one of our floats (which had replaced the coal carts) and said that St. Peter would be shocked if he turned up at the Golden Gates riding on a load of hay, he wanted to go to Heaven brandishing a gory sword!

We had 1 or 2 Field days round Highclere, Kingsclere and up on Sidmonton Downs. We were now feeling quite at home in the saddle. On **16th November 1914** we left in a hurry and trained for Sheringham, Norfolk.

We arrived at 6.00 am on a terribly cold morning. We marched off after everybody had had time to get very cold and spent two nights in a filthy barn near Holt.

I remember that Cyril had difficulty with the bacon next morning owing to the curiosity of about 20 young pigs who wanted to see how it was cooked.

We moved off again on the 19th November and marched to Birmingham where General Wiggin had an argument with a farmer who "didn't want a lot of soldiers on his place".

I must say that 'D' Squadron took the starch out of that gentleman before they left his place – the poultry etc. diminished very rapidly!

The dear old MG Sec'n spent the night in a little shed with some dirty straw. Field and Goodson elected to lie under a straw-rick outside but they had so many rats running over their faces that they had to move during the night.

We were glad to see Captain John Lyttleton next morning; he soon found us some decent billets. He split the Sec'n in half at each farm.

I went to Mr Sadlers farm where we had a large barn to ourselves. Whilst there, I had tonsillitis. Mrs Sadler kindly took me in for several nights – it was good to sleep in a bed again. Bert King cooked for our party and did us proud, but it was a very rough life. The weather was bad and our horses started catching cold and needed a lot of attention.

We were very glad of the big open fire that we kept going in the middle of the barn which used to smoke us to death. Practically 'active service' conditions. Our only relaxation was a bit of ferreting and visits to the 'Chequers' at Gresham where we used to get a good cheap supper.

We met the Honourable Artillery Corps (HAC), of whom we saw such a lot on active service, at Gresham.

I looked at my diary and saw that I was due Annual Leave about now. I don't think that choosing Barningum for leave was a good idea. We went on several trips to Cromer (overrated, in my opinion). Perhaps the fact that it was November made it seem uninteresting. We dug a few trenches on the cliffs at Runcton but did not use them as on **11th December 1914** we marched off through Melton Constable to Dunton near Fakenham.

We spent another night on straw in an old barn, then on again to **Kings Lynn**, a very depressing looking little old fashioned sea port town.

First impressions of Kings Lynn were far from favourable, but before we left we found our way to its best side. In the hearts of all Worcester Yeomen, Kings Lynn still holds the chief place amongst the towns where we did our training.

The inhabitants of Kings Lynn all seemed involved with the one idea of making us enjoy ourselves. Although we put in some very hard work, we also did plenty of playing.

The fact that Kings Lynn was the last town in England that we saw anything of, did put a halo round it when viewed from 3,000 miles away!

I cannot say enough about the kindness and warm welcome we had from the townsfolk. At Kings Lynn we soon settled down to real hard training.

Each morning the Regiment marched out to Middleton for riding school, sword practice, troop drill and other work that we would need later on in the desert. We, in the MG Sec'n, had a change of Officers.

Lieutenant Colville taking over from Lieutenant Watts, I believe, was a change for the better. The first thing that 'Johnny' did was to teach us how to handle and use the Maxim guns which was rather essential.

I was sent on an MG course to Bisley and had a good fortnight with Ernest Hickman of the Warwick's who was unfortunately killed on Gallipoli.

I came back a full blown Instructor. Johnny soon gave me plenty to do with the result that we taught everybody in the Sec'n all we knew before we sailed east.

The horses were in good stabling, they had plenty of food and attention. I am perfectly sure that there was not a smarter or better drilled Cavalry Regiment in the Army as we departed England. In the spring, our Divisional General, General Payton, inspected us and was very complimentary.

The chief reason, of course, was that our horses were by now well trained and knew what was expected of them, which every cavalry man knows is half the battle.

During this strenuous training period, the brighter side of life was not forgotten, our evenings being one continuous round of enjoyment.

The many ways of spending them were too numerous to mention. All Kings Lynn doors were 'open' to us; our main trouble was that we had too many invitations at once.

My main form of entertainment was tea at the Conservative Club, followed by snooker all evening with Cyril, Shorty and Goodson plus a few others.

The club members were all good to us and organised concerts, tripe suppers and other forms of entertainment. The old Major performing his famous song, I shall never forget.

Shorty distinguished himself by falling in love, at least that is what he told us, but I had grave suspicions that his fiancée's pork pies were the attraction (she being the daughter of a pork butcher!).

Several of our boys were smitten at Kings Lynn. I heard that quite a number returned to redeem promises made on moonlit nights in the 'walks' or up the Middleton Road.

I could write many pages of happenings at Kings Lynn (the first Zeppelin raid over England (see photo), manoeuvres on the surrounding country, the review in Sandringham Park.

My visit with Cyril to Sandringham House, stables etc machine gun practice at the mouth of the Ouse, exercises to places 15-20 miles distance and evenings at the Conservative Club etc but must hasten or my reader will think that I am never going to sail away to fight. A spectacle took place at Kings Lynn before we left that would have thrilled any cavalry man.

A Regimental Parade (mounted) in the market square – 300 men and horses took part, spit and polish all round, never looked better. Lieutenant Colonel the Earl of Dudley addressed us from the balcony of the Town Hall telling us that we were to go on Active Service soon.

He expected every man to acquit himself as Worcestershire Yeomen had always done in the past.

13 - *1ˢᵗ German bomb dropped on UK by a Zeppelin (Kings Lynn Jan 1915)*

12A - SS Saturnia in the Mediterranean (April 1915)

Chapter 4

Overseas on Active Service (1915)

We departed Kings Lynn at 4.00 pm on **8th April 1915** for Avonmouth and arrived there in the middle of the night. We immediately loaded our horses on to the "Eloby".

The soldiers boarded the "SS Saturnia" and set sail around 4.00 pm on the 11th April. We soon discovered that we were not considered 'First Class' passengers and we learnt the art of sleeping in a hammock. The ship was overcrowded, the food atrocious.

I often wondered how many millions Messrs Donaldson & Co (and other shipping companies) made by starving and overcrowding the men who had volunteered to defend England.

15 - The Starvation Troopship (SS Saturnia) April 1

Avonmouth to Alexandria

Our first stop was at Clevedon where a TPD (HMS Llewellyn) came alongside. We took advantage of this by climbing over the bulwarks and exploring the destroyer where the sailors showed us everything of interest.

We turned in safe in the knowledge that HMS Llewellyn was escorting us for about 100 miles. We woke in the morning and found that we were out of sight of land.

The ship had a good roll; consequently nasty noises were going on all around us.

It was not long before I lost interest. Whilst in this unfortunate condition I was dragged up on to the poop by Lieutenant Colville to give him the benefit of my advice on fixing up our MGs to defend the ship (this was before the days when transporters carried quickly firing guns).

Needless to say I took very little interest in the proceedings and I should not have cared if they had thrown the guns overboard!

The days became monotonous and we spent our time playing cards. The only blessing was the beautiful weather (not supplied by Donaldson & Co!).

The first land we saw was Gibraltar. The searchlights examined us very carefully as we passed by in the dark. On the 17th April we sighted the snow-capped mountains of Spain and on the 18th April, the Algerian coast.

After our entry into the Mediterranean, most of us spent the nights on deck as the weather were very mild. On the 19th April we coasted Tunisia and on the 20th April we arrived at **Malta**.

On entering the Grand Harbour we passed several French battle ships which turned out their bands to play us in (Jules Ferry, Danton, Courbet and an old British ship, the Caesar).

We responded with the Marseillaise, Tipperary etc. in about a dozen different keys (unaccompanied).

In the afternoon we had permission to go ashore and had the most enjoyable time. We heard that Lord Windsor, who was on the Governor's staff obtained this privilege for us.

Everybody's first thought was to have a good square meal as we were half starved. We had a meal at one restaurant, promptly followed by another meal at a different restaurant.

Malta was a lovely place. The harbour is surrounded with hills on which is built the town of Valetta. In the town the first thing we noticed were the peculiar hoods (Ghonella) the women wore.

A large affair which they swung in front of their faces when they did not wish to be stared at.

Down the peculiar little streets (all hills) women sit at their doors making the famous lace. Herds of goats are all about the place, you get your milk straight from the animal.

No adulteration here, a veritable happy hunting ground for curio seekers. The men of Malta are very much like Italians, they look like a lot of cut-throats. You have to keep your eyes open at night in this delightful little island.

We departed the following day played out by the French men and with three submarines coming into harbour. On the 24th April we awoke to find we were outside Alexandria.

Chapter 5

City of Alexandria (1915) Seen from the sea it is rather unimpressive owing to the flatness of the country. The famous lighthouse of Ras-El-Tin towers above everything else.

One is struck right away by the absence of chimneys and roofs. Away to the west is desert - bright yellow with palm trees. One feels that here at last, is the Orient.

We were terribly anxious to bid farewell to our transport. We were ashore at last and did a March through the City in full kit (thick Serge) on a very hot day.

Our first idea of the City was what we saw in the native quarters near the Docks – filth everywhere. When we progressed and reached the European area we discovered a different City altogether, reminding us of a nice French town.

Indeed, French influence was seen everywhere in the street names, advertisements, tradesmen's signs, all in French – one looked in vain for a bit of English!

We arrived at last at our camp, Chatby, and found that the horses had arrived the day before. We lost 26 animals on the voyage which I suppose was not excessive. Chatby was in a lovely position right on the edge of the sea with trains running close by.

We discovered that grass did not grow in Egypt; consequently our camp was soon very dusty.

When the wind blew, one could not see 100 yards. We decided to explore this wonderful, wicked City. I should mention that we first had to raise the 'wind' from a sympathetic Officer, Lord Hampton, as we were all 'broke'.

The Piasters were a little strange at first. We were done down several times, but we soon got the hang of them.

We found Alexandria a nice City, if we kept to the European half. It was not long before we found a French restaurant where we could have a 5-course dinner with a bottle of Vin Rouge thrown in for 2/-. Most of our evenings commenced there!

As already mentioned, the European quarter is very French. The streets are well kept with high blocks of buildings on each side. In the centre of the City is Consuls Square with a large equestrian statue of Mohammed Ali.

This marks the place where a few thousand Alexandrians were massacred about 50 years previous. The Bourse (or Exchange) is a good looking building. Shereef Pasha Street has some very fine shops.

If you cross the big square you will find yourself in a very different quarter. The famous Rue de Soeurs (Sister Street) leads into the heart of the native quarter. Some of our boys called it "Rue de Sewers" which was really quite appropriate!

This district was one compact mass of low cafes where they sell 'poison' and call it whiskey, where nasty Arab eating houses stink of olive oil and garlic and where brothels abound with horrible painted women of all nationalities (except English) who shriek at you from their doorsteps, balconies or bedrooms.

Thieves thrive, with murderers and blackguards of all descriptions and nations. I shall never forget my first visit to this quarter with Cyril, Bylie and Tiger.

It seemed too strange to be true. I could not have believed that such a place existed. We were glad to get away at last and breathe some good, clean fresh air.

Whilst at Chatby we worked at drill of all descriptions for the first month or so, for we quite expected to be sent to the Gallipoli Peninsula, as the famous landing had been made the day after our arrival at Alexandria (**25th April 1915**).

16 - Alexandria: a small street in the French / European Quarter
Note: The Muslim women shopping in the street, probably wives of wealthy men

17 - Bazaar in native Quarter: note the Fez on the men

As time went on the weather became hotter, we could do very little during the day except bathe. Exercising horses of course had to be done every day.

This took place before breakfast and the route we followed was along the Mahmoudin Canal which connects Alexandria with the Nile, then round Mouzha Gardens – a beautifully kept public park where they actually grew good grazing grass.

One evening in May, Cyril and myself visited a French Fete "Pour la Croix Rouge" in the Jardins Rosette, where they obtained some wonderful effects at night with lanterns suspended from the palms, a very pretty show. In early June, Cyril, Bylie and I managed to get weekend leave and visited Cairo.

Chapter 6

City of Cairo (1915)

We had an excellent train journey lasting 3½ hours travelling 2nd class which is about equal to our Midland 3rd class! Passing through Lower Egypt, which is, I suppose, one of the most productive lands in the World, canals everywhere, not much wasteland.

The whole country is arable with some wonderful crops grown. Most of the land is cultivated with sugar-cane and cotton plus barley, maize and millet. Tomatoes and wheat are also grown in good quantities – but one misses the green fields of home.

The native villages are generally built on a slight eminence, so as to be above the floods when Father Nile overflows.

They are just a collection of mud huts with roofs of reeds and grass all jammed tightly together. The country is as flat as our Fen land. The railway runs along a built-up embankment so one has a very good view of the surrounding country.

We arrived at Cairo and were met by Mr Chinn, a friend of Cyril's Father who immediately took us under his wing and gave us a good weekend at his flat near the Abdin Palace.

17A – Sightseeing in Cairo on Camels, Godrich on the left

The Pyramids and Sphinx were, of course, our first objective. It was very lucky for us that they built Cairo within easy reach of them or we should never have got there.

They are about 10 miles out and one can get there on a tram from the centre of Cairo which takes you to within half a mile of the Great Pyramid for 2½d (civilians 5d).

No profit in that! The Tramway runs along a road raised above the surrounding country (same reason as the railway) with an avenue of trees the whole distance (said to be built in honour of a visit by the Empress Eugenie to a former Khedive).

When we arrived at the tram terminus, we were met by swarms of guides, curio sellers, donkey boys, ice cream vendors etc. We fought our way to the camels and hired one of these intelligent beasts each.

We mounted for our first ride on this "ship of the desert". It is a wonderful experience; you throw a leg over the saddle and wonder if the driver will ever wake the lazy looking beast.

While you are pondering this, you are suddenly pitched forward, nearly falling off, then you are thrown violently right to the back of the saddle, another slight jolt from the rear and you perceive that the beast is "up" with you high in the World – it looks a long way to fall. We found camel riding very comfortable, but after a long ride your back gets very sore, owing to the continuous rocking to and fro.

We climbed uphill about half a mile and arrived on the sand at the foot of the Great Pyramid of Cheops, which is appropriately enough, nearest to Cairo – it is the largest of all the Pyramids. The first impression is a huge mountain of stone, consisting of little steps up which it looks possible to run, but when you get near to them; you find that they are five feet high.

Looking up to the top you will see little ants (visitors) waving what appear to be postage stamps. As a contrast to the age of the old Pyramids, I was surprised to see a wireless aerial suspended between a high mast and the top of the Great Pyramid. This edifice, the Great Pyramid, I was told afterwards, is 480 feet high, its sides 700 feet long. It is so big you cannot persuade yourself that it was built by human hands. One keeps regarding it as a peculiar shaped hill. We were invited by several Arabs to climb to the top, they offered to pull us all the way for about 6d and deliver you safe and sound again at the bottom. As it was a hot day, we

declined as we had quite a good view of Cairo from the camels, so
we said 'Maleesh' which means 'Sanfarien'.

On our tour of inspection round the mountain we observed a little
hole in the side of the Pyramid with several small figures about it.

This suggested a trip inside which we immediately jumped at,
dismounted and climbed up to the doorway where our guide told
us to take our boots off.

We knew that boots were not allowed in Mosques, but did not see
the connection between the Pyramids and the Mahomedan religion.

The old Arab pointed to the floor inside which was Alabaster,
polished by the feet of thousands of visitors, so we sat down and
removed our boots. I was very glad we did, as inside the passage
runs in inclines, first a steep downward slope then a steep upwards
incline and so on. The polished floor makes it almost impossible
to stand upright in heavy boots. The passage is about six feet high;
my head was frequently in trouble. We arrived at the centre of the
building, at last, lit by a torch carried by our guide.

We found ourselves in a huge chamber, empty except for a large
stone coffin in the centre. This is called the King's Chamber,
underneath is a similar room named the Queen's Chamber.

A large number of 'Mummies' were found here some years ago
when the doorway was discovered, they can be seen in the Cairo
Museum. We next went on to the Sphinx which is close by. The
expression on the face of this huge statue is very puzzling, despite
the damage done to it.

It lies below the level of the surrounding desert, due to the sand
blowing up continually. It was dug out some years ago.

Close by the Sphinx is the Temple of the Sphinx, said to have been
dedicated to the worship of the wonderful statue nearby. This also
lies below the level of the desert so one has to descend a flight of
stone steps.

At the ground floor of the Temple there are huge blocks of granite,
oblong in shape, standing on end with similar oblong blocks laid
across to form an avenue. The walls are also formed of these
tremendous blocks of stone, some as long as the walls of an
ordinary living room all cut in different shapes and sizes and fitted
perfectly together. The corners of this strange building are formed
not by two blocks being placed at right angles to each other, but by
one block being cut out in the shape of a right angle. We were
shown several recesses (believed to be tombs of Priests), made of
Alabaster, which reflect millions of lights on a match being lit and
held inside. We saw many other interesting details.

*18 - Chatby Camp: Alexandria June 1915 – Spare time hobby by MG Sec'n
Emblems (left to right) are: Warwickshire:Gloucstershire: Worcestershire*

*19 - Corporal E V Godrich: Alexandria (June 1915)
The 3 stripes on the left arm signify either long service or good conduct*

Back outside we looked south and saw the Pyramids of Sakhara. To the west is nothing but sand hills and valleys, all the same monotonous colour.

To the north was Mena Camp which the Australians had just vacated for Gallipoli. Finally, to the east was the valley of the Nile looking green and prosperous with Cairo in the middle distance – a white city with the Citadel standing over it like a protector, with the red hills of Mokattam in the background.

This view at sunset is surely one of the most wonderful in the World. The contrast between the white City and the deep red of the hills is too vivid to describe. If seen in a picture, the average person would call it absurd.

When standing at this vantage point, you can appreciate the value of the Nile to Egypt. It is possible to mark just where the flood water reaches every year. Up to this point the soil is black and will grow any crop (the soil is similar to the English Fens). Beyond the high water mark it is bright yellow sand which stretches west for hundreds of miles and nothing grows except Palm trees in occasional patches.

The Mousky was our next trip; this is the old Arab market of the City. The district does a good trade, not only in native requirements but also in curios, silks, carpets etc. shipped to Europe. The area consists of narrow streets, each street containing some sort of industry. The first we explored was the Gold Bazaar; this is so narrow that two people cannot walk abreast.

On each side are little shops, practically only cupboards in the wall! The proprietors sit cross-legged by the side of their showcase and fashion gold into ladies ornaments etc.

They look a half-witted, lazy lot but you only have to stop and look like buying something and you soon realise that they are quite aware of 'how many beans make five'. Many of them can bargain in quite good English. Then there is the precious stones bazaar, but the most interesting of all is the brass industries.

You can see the native workmen busy with small hammers and chisels cutting weird designs on trays, gongs and other brass articles. The noise is overpowering, the smell in the Bazaar speaks for itself. Amongst the small shops and stalls, you occasionally come to the entrance of a large business. Upon entering you find yourself in a wonderful place surrounded by eastern workmanship in all forms – carpets, brass work, woodwork etc.

These larger shops generally belong to Jewish or Indian firms; many have branches in London, Paris etc. The counter men are always very smart and could talk some of our commercial travellers to a standstill. They always start by serving coffee

I remember a young man in one of these shops commencing the business by confiding in us that he was exceptionally keen on everything English.

His one ambition was to marry an English girl, and he asked, how much did we think he ought to save before he travelled to England to find a wife? After a heart to heart talk, we felt we had to buy esomething.

These firms are very enterprising, we made our purchase and left the name and address of our friend at home to whom the parcel was to be sent. By paying a small insurance fee (about 1d) they would guarantee to send another similar parcel if the first was lost by submarine action. Torpedoing was an everyday occurrence in the Mediterranean. I am pleased to relate that all our purchases arrived home safely without the test of the firm's honesty.

In the evening we explored the Wagh El Berka, Clot Bey and other parts of the Ezbekieh district which we found weird, wonderful and far-surpassing anything we had seen at Alexandria. Ezbekieh Gardens, situated in the centre of the City, were really well kept. You could retire there to a shady nook; feast yourself on ice-cream with a treat for the eyes in the shape of a beautifully kept lawn – a little bit of heaven in the midst of this great noisy, dusty and wicked City.

The museums at Cairo are well worth a visit. The contents are set out in an exceptionally clear manner. The labels are in English, French and Arabic.

The exhibits are practically all ancient relics of old Egypt, which of course you would expect. I was most interested in the Mummy of Ptolemy the Great. One can look at the actual features of the man who scowled on the Jews and ordered that they be cleared out of Egypt thousands of years ago. The lapse of time is too great to realise. The Norman relics of England impress me just as much.

These remnants of a civilisation that was dead and buried when Rome was flourishing, proves the old saying that, "there is nothing new under the sun".

We were shown gold rings, necklaces and bangles that would not look out of place in a modern ballroom.

Chapter 7

The Citadel (1915)

The Citadel is a huge Fort which stands on an eminence and completely dominates Cairo. Unlike the majority of Forts, it is not ugly. The highest part of it is surmounted by a beautiful Mosque dedicated to Mohammed Ali (the last of the Egyptian rulers when she was an independent nation).

The Mosque is crowned by a large dome; on either side are two very high thin Minarets which give a beautiful finish to the whole place. The interior is completely covered with Alabaster and is lit by hundreds of lights in huge chandeliers, which must give it a semblance to Fairyland when illuminated. Inside the walls of the Fort are a large Hospital, Barracks, Prison and living quarters for numerous married soldiers. Many strange stories are told about the old place. The best known is the Massacre of the Mamelukes.

These were the Noblemen of Egypt about 300 years ago. It is related to one Sultan who, getting wind of a plot amongst these gentlemen, invited them all to the Citadel to a grand feast.

When he had them all in a courtyard, he let loose his soldiers; they were all murdered with the exception of one who escaped by mounting his horse, jumping the wall and dropping about 100 feet down the rock. The horse was killed (his hoof mark is still shown to visitors, for a small charge, of course).

From the top of the Citadel walls is obtained one of the finest views in the World. In the foreground is the Mousky district which is as thick with Mosques and Minarets as Birmingham is with chimney stacks.

This huge City is spread out for miles in all directions. The white houses with flat roofs have a very pleasing appearance. The Nile is a straight line of silver cutting the landscape in two. In the background are the Pyramids and Sphinx with the yellow desert spreading out behind. This view at sunset plus the one from the Pyramids, I shall always remember.

We completed our visit to Cairo with dinner in one of the very fine restaurants which abound. We had a whiskey and soda on the veranda at Shepheards Hotel, one of the most famous hotels in the World. We went home by donkey and found our spurs very useful, despite the boy's entreaties, "no spike in mister".

Cyril won an exciting race by about 10 lengths. I shall always maintain that it was because his legs were shorter than mine, which unfortunately hampered my donkey.

Back with the regiment at Alexandria, we noticed the cool sea breezes, which would have been appreciated at Cairo. Europeans always migrate to the seaside for the hot months. It is extraordinary what a difference 150 miles can make to the temperature.

On one occasion we had a Field Day near the camp, without our horses. I was fortunate enough to occupy the roof of a large house with my machine gun. This turned out to be the residence of a Mr Roy, a Birmingham man – this introduction led to a series of pleasant evenings in good old English style. We also had a few interesting visits to the camp of some French Cavalry, the Chasseurs D'Afrique, who hailed from Morocco. They always seemed to have a good flow of Vin Rouge whenever we called.

About this time Austin Woodward had an attack of Measles and in spite of a good send off, went away feeling very dejected.

8ᵗʰ May 1915: General Maxwell O/C Troops inspected us in the Rue Rosette. We did a 'posh' Cavalry march-past (I suspect for the benefit of the native spectators). We also saw our first Turks, a boat-load of prisoners who had arrived from the Dardanelles. We met and escorted them to the railway station – from there they were sent to Cairo. They struck me as a well-made lot of fellows who would give a good account of themselves.

29ᵗʰ May 1915: Spent the afternoon with Sam Banister, George Smith and Cyril in Mouzha Gardens. In the evening we went to a French fete.

10ᵗʰ June 1915: I went to Ras El Tin with Cyril and visited 'Slim' Field) who was 6ft 4" in height) in hospital. There we met Harry Enefer, McDonald, Welsh and Ern Sales who took us up the famous Ras El Tin Lighthouse. They were all Birmingham men serving in RE Signals.

16ᵗʰ to 18ᵗʰ June 1915: The Khamseen Wind was blowing like a furnace. Everything you touch burns your hands; clothes (shorts and shirt) weigh a ton.

Everybody very fed up. Poor old Shorty was "run in" for insubordination and sent to Cairo for 3 weeks. We all swore vengeance on Colville (who at the time was himself sickening with hepatitis, although we only discovered this later).

25th June 1915: A party of us was sent to the end of the breakwater with guns to defend the entrance to the harbour in case of submarine attack.
This was a real snip as we spent most of our time fishing and swimming. It was a great change from our dusty old camp.

28th June 1915: Night scheme out to Sidi Bish. The '**D**' Squadron went badly astray. I had a strong argument with Lieutenant Ward which was settled by Lord Hampton. Arrived back at camp about 8.00 am very fed up and too hot to sleep.

2nd July 1915: We left Chatby for a 12 mile march to Aboukir, right in the desert but on the coast. Here we had a strenuous fortnight with very little grub. Drill every morning from 4.00 am till 8.00 am, talk about getting an appetite for breakfast! We found the surrounding countryside very beautiful.
Aboukir Bay had nice clean sand and a fringe of palm trees with lovely bathing. This was where Nelson fought one of his famous victories over Napoleon's navy. Colville left us with jaundice about the fourth day, so things eased up a little.
We finished our stay at Aboukir with swimming sports. Jack Palethorpe was Champion of the Regiment, Jack Knight and Eddie Williams were also very good. One memory of Aboukir will be of its snakes, scorpions and centipedes – these horrible beasts were numerous, frequently finding them in our blankets when we rose.

Back at Chatby, Colville was sent up to Kom El Dic Fort for the benefit of his health. Pikey Adams, with seven men, was sent to the breakwater and the few of us left had plenty to do with the spare horses.

24th July 1915: An accident occurred that affected everybody. Billy Somers unfortunately suffered heart trouble whilst swimming and was drowned before he could be saved. Billy was our first casualty and being a popular old chap, his loss was felt by all. He was buried on 25th July in the English Cemetery at Chatby. Cyril and I attended, plus the Colonel and Captain Wiggin were also present.

30th July 1915: Another wretched night scheme to Sidi Bish, consisting principally of digging trenches all night long!

1st August 1915: Cyril and I set off for morning service at the English Church. It was a sweltering day so we called in at the French restaurant for an iced drink and stayed for lunch instead of attending Church. Various rumours were going round and we suddenly began bayonet exercises, of which we were in ignorance owing to our cavalry training.
We guessed that our first experience of War would be as Infantry and our destination we anticipated would be Gallipoli. Alexandria was the base for the Dardanelles operations. We constantly saw drafts of reinforcements leaving for the ill-fated peninsula.
We now began to see another side of the story as parties of our men were sent down to the Docks to help unload wounded men who were constantly arriving.

These gallant chaps were packed into any old 'tub' available, many of them had the original bandage that was placed there when they received their first 'hit' five or six days previous. This was a horrible job, frequently we discovered a corpse lying between two live men. It was a good thing that the conditions that these first men on Gallipoli fought under were never made known in England or probably a few more careers would have been wrecked.

I have heard the peninsula described as a shambles. It undoubtedly was. All these sights impressed us, but I can honestly say that they did not dampen our enthusiasm to get into the 'business' ourselves. I could tell the story of many an argument and many a 'wrangle' to get on the boat when we did eventually sail.

8th August 1915: Percy Cheston was invalided home with jaundice – very sorry to lose him as he was a real worker – quite a 'rough diamond'.
A day or two later, Bousfield (Bussy) went into Hospital for an operation for his varicose veins – Diakonesse, a German Hospital with German Nurses. We went to see him and found him to be comfortable – the Nurses most obliging. 'Bussy' was afterwards sent to Cyprus to recuperate, so he missed the Peninsula. He was killed at Katia in 1916.

Chapter 8

Embarkation for Gallipoli

12th August 1915: We had news at last that we were to take part in the War and were to sail on 14th August. During the day we received an issue of webbing equipment (Infantry). It was supplied in about 20 pieces and as it was new to us Cavalry men, we had great fun assembling it – a case of 'trial and error'!

13th August 1915: Colville splashed out to the extent of 100 Piasters for drinks all round, but as there were 20 of us to share it; we did not pass the bounds of sobriety for it amounted to the huge sum of 1/- per head. The day was spent in preparation – medical inspections and deciding who was to stay with the horses etc. In the evening the MG Section adjourned to the French restaurant, which had always treated us well, for a farewell dinner.
The proprietor, a fat old French lady, occupied herself while we were feeding and sewing our blue patches on our tunics.
This merry little party finished up at the Cap d'Or café, which proved to be the last one with several of the company.

14th August 1915: Early Reveille spent hours trying to pack our valises leaving all un-necessaries in our kit bags etc.
What a terrible lump this pack is on one's back. Goodbye to Marshall Harris, Ted Poole, Bert Kings and Alf Daw who were "told off" to stay with the horses. Parade about 11.00 am in full Infantry marching order for the first time, and then moved to the Docks. It was a real Egyptian day, hot as blazes.
The four miles to the Docks nearly killed some of us for we were not only in Infantry kit but also wearing thick khaki serge.
We embarked on the Cunard liner "Ascania" and sailed about 6.00 pm. The next day at sea was uneventful, but awfully hot below decks, everybody sleeping on deck. Discovered T. Weaver and Trinder were on same boat.

16th August 1915: Passing the islands of Greece which look very beautiful from the distance we viewed them. It struck me that it would be a nasty part of the World for a sailor to get lost in as we threaded our way in-between little islands that rose up straight from the sea to a tremendous height.

17th August 1915: We arrived at the island of Mudros and entered the great harbour of Lemnos, a wonderful natural deep water harbour. It was appropriated by the British Navy with their usual impudence. This island and harbour were extremely useful to us as an advanced base during the Peninsula Campaign.

It was very close to the landing places that had been captured and was safe from submarine attacks. The harbour was full of ships of all sizes, the battleships, Lord Nelson and Prince George, the old cruiser, Cornwallis, the liner, Royal George, were a few I noted.

10 B - The harbour at Lemnos

The Royal George was a sister ship of Royal Edward which was torpedoed a few miles from Lemnos the day before we arrived. The Royal Edward was loaded principally with hospital requisites – x-ray apparatus, medicines etc.

It carried a large number of Nurses and RAMC personnel, many of whom were drowned. It was a severe blow to our Dardanelles Operation and the effects were felt for months afterwards when the bad weather arrived.

Lemnos became a huge graveyard, many of the lads who had been wounded on the peninsula, died here from lack of attention or food. I am sorry to say that many of the brave nursing women died also. After remaining on the "Ascania" all day, we transferred to the Queen Victoria, a small paddle steamer that used to run tourists down the Thames to Margate.

Chapter 9

Gallipoli (1915)

It was War Minister Lord Kitchener's idea to despatch land forces to the Gallipoli peninsula to help the Navy proceed through the narrows of the Dardanelles. These Straits are about 40 miles long and some parts are about 3-5 miles wide.

Warships sailing through this passage were sunk by floating mines laid down from Cannakale on the Eastern shore making it impossible for the navy to have a safe entry into the Straits.

On both sides of the straits there were heavy Turkish guns some from Germany which could not be neutralised by naval gunfire alone and would make it unwise to continue forcing through this plan.

The only solution was to silence the guns on both sides of the Straits and to let the navy safe passage through after the mine sweepers cleaned the area.

Admiral Sackville Carden, commander of the British naval squadron also had sent a message to Sir Winston Churchill and Lord Kitchener saying that Dardanelles is impossible to be conquered soon without the help of ground expeditionary forces.

But unfortunately the move was not quick enough and the successive Allied forces suffered heavy casualties. Strong opposition, disease and winter misery of rain and frost led to the abandonment of the Dardanelle expedition.

We left Lemnos at 5.00 pm and after a pleasant little run, on which we passed scores of dead horses and wreckage of all sorts, we arrived in Suvla Bay.

We were landed from the Queen Victoria in small barges on to a little wooden jetty that had been built a day or two before. The whole operation was carried out by the Navy.

It was now 1.00 am and pitch-dark, for which we ought to have been thankful. But to us, fighting seemed a long way off as we had a nice peaceful night.

We had no idea that we were in easy reach of the Turkish guns – we rather resented the order "No Smoking".

As we got ashore and up the beach, the first thing I remember was the peculiar smell which I shall remember all my life when I think of Gallipoli. It is the scrub that grows out east, mixed with the smell of death. I can recall that same smell again at Gaza, Beersheba, Kuwelfeh, Es Salt and several places where men had been killed.

There is nothing like the sense of smell to refresh one's memory – that peculiar Gallipoli smell I shall always carry in my memory.
We were lucky to have a clear landing. The 54th Division (London Territorial) had landed under heavy fire and had swept 'Johnny Turk' inland about a week previously, but due to heavy losses, were unable to push their initial successes home. Apparently there was a shortage of Infantry, so we were brought in to try our luck.
We spent the remainder of that first night about 300 yards from where we came ashore, but did not sleep much owing to the strange noises going on all round us.

At dawn we were up and looking for some wood to light a fire for a brew of tea. We discovered that we were on the shores of a fine bay with a beautiful panorama. The bay was full of ships, battle ships, hospital ships, transports etc with a good view of the coast south to Anzac Cove. Inland, the hills rose up to 800 feet, on the top of which 'Johnny Turk' was an interested spectator of our activities.
About 6.00 am he showed that he disapproved of the landing of another Division by sending over a few fire crackers.
I must confess that at the first taste of shell fire, I felt very funky and wanted to find a hole anywhere out of the road but there was nowhere to go! The Turks began shelling the rest of our regiment who were coming ashore in barges. By watching men who had been ashore a few days, one gained confidence.
It was easy to pick out the new arrivals, men like myself. When a 5.9 dropped, one ducked by instinct at an explosion. We soon got tired of flattening ourselves each time we heard the whistle of a shell coming over.
Hunger and thirst soon asserted themselves. In addition, there is always that irresistible human curiosity so excellently expressed by Captain Bairnsfather "where did that one go Bill?"
I have seen fine speeches, sermons, court martials, men writing letters to their sweethearts, all interrupted by a bursting shell or bomb (even when they have been a mile away) just to see the result of the explosion.

20 cc- Yeomanry advancing frontal attack under shellfire

SOLDIERS CROSSING THE SALT LAKE AT SUVLA
From the painting by Norman Wilkinson
(Reproduced by permission of the Imperial War Museum)

20A - Yeomanry Division Frontal Attack

Our own particular Officer, Colville (who was a terrible fire-eater in England) distinguished himself very early by digging a good 'dug-out' and staying in it. He became the ridicule of all of us.

I remember him exhorting us on one occasion to 'duck'. "I believe in ducking, my family always ducked" became a password in the MG Section.

Our first day in Gallipoli was mostly spent in fatigues, straightening out our kit, ammunition, tools, scrounging for wood for a fire etc.

The shelling carried on intermittently all day and was occasionally replied to by one of the battleships that were lying off the coast.

Several Warwick boys were hit by a shell whilst on water fatigue. Jim Hewings came back from the well with a tale of a shell that had burst 2 yards from him and had only scratched his leg, but the 'sceptics' told him that he had scratched himself whilst bathing on a rock!

At about 7.00 pm whilst we were seeing to our first rum ration, two Taubes came over. We were interested watching the battle ships trying to hit them with shrapnel.

Altogether it was a crowded day, the little incidents seem trivial now in the light of future events, but I think first impressions in most walks of life are generally the most lasting.

19th August 1915: Tiger and I spent most of the day trying to enlarge our dug-out which was about six inches deep. Being on a sloping hill was not good.

Parties were continually coming down from the trenches for rations; water and ammo, which all had to be carried uphill paths for about 3 miles in blazing sunshine.

We bathed on 'A' beach which was constantly interrupted by 'Johnny' shelling us.

I remember one funny incident when a rather fat Quartermaster, who was enjoying a bathe, was standing up to his knees in water and dressed in his birthday suit (costumes were not de rigueur on Gallipoli), when a shell dropped in the water a few hundred yards away from him.

Luckily it did not explode or my story would have ended differently. The fat man's face was a picture of amazement. He hurried ashore over some sharp rocks, apparently preferring a shell on dry land.

20th August 1915: We spent the day getting ready for a night march and were much relieved when we heard that our "packs" were to be left behind.

We now had all our worldly possessions in our pockets and haversacks, we even left our greatcoats behind. At night fall we moved off and trekked round the shores of Suvla Bay to a hill we called Haji Baba (Hadji or Achi Baba).

We had a gruelling time as we had to carry all our guns and ammo the whole distance – most of it across soft sand.

We arrived at last and dropped down, dead-beat, close to what we thought were wagons. We soon fell asleep but were awakened by a terrific explosion quite near.

Thinking that the Turks had got our range with some big guns, we sprang up in alarm. We soon realised that we were lying close to a battery of 18 pounders who were firing a few rounds.

At daybreak we were up and digging-in again. As no fires were allowed, we had a jolly breakfast of 'bully & biscuits' (with cold water) and then tried to return to our sleep.

Chapter 10

Baptism of Fire 21st August 1915

At 2.00 pm the whole division was paraded while a terrific bombardment from the battleships and guns ashore was in progress. They pumped hundreds of shells at the Turks. As there was no response, we thought that all the Turkish guns had been knocked out. At 3.00 pm we moved off, it was a beautiful Saturday afternoon.

Whilst waiting for the Order to Advance, my thoughts flew to Sparkhill. I could picture the happy people at home going out into the country on their bikes, driving their cars etc.

I wondered if I should ever see Stratford Road again. I learned afterwards that my sister Winnie was enjoying herself at a wedding at about the same time.

We advanced in Columns of Troops across an open plain with hills about two miles ahead.

Our objective was a good sized hill which was named Chocolate Hill due to its dark brown colour. All went well till the leading brigade (Sherwoods, South Notts and Derby's) got halfway across the plain, then all hell was let loose.

Shrapnel fell like hail, rifle fire like rain made gaps in our ranks. It was not a pleasant feeling to see a man dropping ahead of you knowing that you would soon be amongst it.

The two miles or so that we marched seemed the longest that I have ever travelled. Every second was a nightmare. We machine gunners could not hurry owing to the heavy loads we were struggling under.

We came across several poor chaps who had finished their soldiering; they looked as though they were asleep. I met Billy Cruse returning with his thumb knocked off.

21 - Chocolate Hill

We passed Captain Russell lying in a pool of blood from a nasty wound in his thigh.

He was laughing all over his face. As we passed him he waved and told us to keep 'well extended' – he was a gentleman and a good soldier. I remember thinking, amid all the noise, what a lot of things needed picking up – helmets, rifles, equipment. Some of the sights we saw were horrible most of the damage from shrapnel or high explosive shells.

To see a man hit by flying, jagged pieces of steel is terrible. I shall never forget a small fellow of the South Notts Yeomanry.

He had been hit across the knuckles by a piece of shell completely smashing his fingers. He was about 17 or 18 and was very upset because he had lost his rifle.

I bandaged his hand to stem the bleeding and told him to make for the hospital. Halfway across, the scrub caught fire. The stretcher bearers had to get busy to save the wounded. I believe several were burnt to death.

At last we arrived in a ravine at the foot of Chocolate Hill where we sheltered from the enemy, and had a much needed rest.

Many enquiries were made for pals; we found our regiment had
fared reasonably well. Billy Clitheroe was the only man in our
Sec'n hit – a piece of shrapnel in the thigh.

Bill wanted to carry on but had to be "ordered off" before he
would leave; such was the spirit in those early days.

After a breather and a 'pull' at our water bottles, we moved off up
the hill. As soon as we reached the top we came under heavy fire
and sustained many casualties.

I saw a few, Allan Hoskins, Bill Davenall and 'Stevo' shot through
the mouth, Frank Burson (the old trumpet Major) in the arm and
George Rushworth in the shoulder.

When we arrived at the top, we dropped into trenches dug by the
Sussex a few days before.

It was now nightfall; the Division seemed to have got rather out of
hand. The 2nd Brigade (Bucks, Berks and Dorset Yeomanry) went
over the left shoulder of Chocolate Hill and attacked Scimitar Hill
which they carried but found themselves enfiladed from both sides
and had to withdraw, losing about two-thirds of their strength.

22 - Life in the Trenches (E.V. Godrich 2nd from right)

Their Brigadier, the Earl of Longford, fell in this action. His body
was never recovered.

Sir John Milbank VC was killed with the Notts.Yeomanry.
Colonel Cole (the old gent who was O/C on the Saturnia) was
crippled for life. Many more well-known men were killed or
wounded on this disastrous day. In the official account of this
battle, Sir Ian Hamilton is very enthusiastic about the way the

Yeoman carried themselves, but as to the actual operations, he is very 'foggy'. It seemed to us that our Officers had gone into action without any clear orders.

One spectacle we saw was of men who had marched two miles under heavy fire, jumping over trenches in which the Infantry were sitting, and then carrying on with the attack.

Everything seemed disjointed. From the official accounts it appears that the Divisional Generals did not carry out General Hamilton's Orders.

We of the Yeomanry Division happened to be the attackers this day and caught it in the neck.

It occurred to us that if the Infantry had co-operated, we might have pushed the Turks right back and in all probability broken through to the high ground commanding the Dardanelles.

But fate was against us, and after floundering about between the British and Turkish trenches all night, we were withdrawn and sent all the way back to the seashore from where we had started the previous afternoon!

22nd August 1915: It was daybreak when we reached the beach again. We were all dead-beat but our first task was to get a little fire going to boil a 'Billy can' of tea, followed by some sleep.

We had about 2 hours rest, and then we were paraded for rifle inspection. It was a very hot day so sleep was almost impossible. There was not a scrap of shade and flies were there in swarms, so we had a bathe. At 7.00 pm we were paraded again in full kit and told we could lie down in ranks until 10.00 pm.

We finally started off again across Chocolate Hill and managed to get there this time without the shrapnel as it was quite dark, but there were plenty of snipers about who seemed to know where we were. On arrival we set about making dug-outs as the hill was quite exposed to the Turkish artillery.

23rd August 1915: During the day digging-in, we learnt a few particulars of Saturday's fight. Out of our Division of 5,000 (Cavalry strength is less than Infantry), we had 1,500 casualties.

The First Brigade lost 60% of their numbers. Of our Brigade, the Gloucester's lost 150 (5 out of 7 Officers), the Warwick's lost 90 and the Worcester's 77.

Captain Russell was missed by everyone in the Brigade. He had a nasty thigh wound, but recovered and later came out to Egypt.

During the day the Turks shelled us which encouraged us to get on with our digging.

At about 6.00 pm we paraded and trekked off into the trenches. This was our first taste of taking up position in the Front Line trenches – up and down, round hundreds of corners (traverses), tumbling over legs of sleeping men, kicking over cans of tea that had taken hours to boil.

I thought we had gone miles but in reality we only went about a mile and a half.

Our first glimpse of trench life was not at all encouraging. Imagine a narrow ditch with sandbags on the side facing the enemy with a dirty, unshaven, hungry looking man about every three yards; little holes in the side of the ditch with a dirty tin over a small fire where some poor devil was trying to make a drink of tea.

The only occupation, sleeping, making tea and standing up as your turn comes to look 'over the top' and watch the enemy. War is a glorious pastime in books when you have the whole scheme laid out, the strategy explained and a map with a red line showing 'our position' marked.

But to the poor beggars 'doing it' there is nothing but misery. One is just a 'unit', your job is to do your turn on the parapet, then get down and sleep (if you can), then you have to start digging or go for a mile or two under fire to fetch water, rations or ammunition.

When we arrived at our destination it was dark and we wanted our machine guns on the parapet. We were shown a dim ridge and told that the enemy was 'over there – range 700 yards'.

The first night, we were naturally very jumpy. Every time the wind rattled the leaves of the bushes, we imagined a Turk attack. Every now and then a rifle would go off, probably a sentry keeping himself awake or to scare the enemy who might be out 'wiring'. Although dead tired, we slept with 'one eye open'.

The following morning we were all able to see our situation better, which is always satisfying! We were attached to the 6th Enniskillen Fusiliers, a rare lot of boys from Belfast mostly.

We also found out that it was good policy to keep your head down if you wanted to keep it intact. The Turkish snipers seemed to get us from all directions, which made it very uncomfortable when you had to get out of the trench for a bit of firewood or for a trip to a latrine. The worst job was fetching water, a journey of half a mile, in very exposed country, to an old Turkish well. The Turks had this place well spotted. As there was always a crowd waiting, they concentrated on it.

The days passed with increasing monotony always awakened at 4.00 am by the sentries who happened to be on at the time. Everybody 'stands to Arms' on the look-out till daybreak.

This is so as to be ready against a surprise attack which generally took place in the dim half-light.

When it is quite light, all but the sentry (1 in every 4) stands down and proceeds to light a fire, boil a can of tea and, if lucky, cook a piece of bacon.

Everyone has a pal with whom he 'mucks-in', shares everything he possesses and if one is on sentry or fetching water, the other gets on with the cooking or something for the comfort of both – real live brotherhood.

The days drag slowly on. The MG Section was isolated from the regiment so we seemed quite alone in the World, although we found one or two very good fellows amongst the Irishmen.

The word was passed down the trench occasionally that Pat or Jock had 'stopped one' and he would not be seen again. This very often happened when some poor chap was filling his pal's water bottle – then the question was "where is my water bottle?" rather than "how is he getting on".

War makes one very callous and inhuman. In the particular position we were at this time, the outlook was ghastly, although we had cleared the ground in front of our trench for about 100 yards or so. 'Jacko' does not bother us so much, but as he was on higher ground, we could see dozens of corpses right up to the Turkish sandbags, many of them black owing to the heather catching fire.

On Tuesday night we heard a faint call of stretcher bearers from 'no-man's land', one or two of the boys went to explore and found a Berkshire Yeoman wounded in the leg, dragging another Yeoman who had been hit in the stomach.

They had both been hit in Saturday's fight and had been out for 3 days and nights. It had taken this fine chap 3 days to drag himself and his pal from near the Turks about 600 yards – a fine example of British pluck.

I learnt afterwards that the hero was Private Potts of the Berkshire Yeomanry. He was awarded the VC (*newspaper cutting*).

GALLIPOLI V.C.S

TWO MORE AWARDS

DEVOTION TO WOUNDED COMRADE.

("Gazette's" Special Service.)

LONDON, Oct. 3.

The "London Gazette" announces tha' the Victoria Cross has been awarded t(Captain P.H. Hansen, of the 6th battalion of the Lincolnshire Regiment, for mos' conspicuous bravery in Gallipoli. Aft ~~~~~~~~~~ Green Knoll. Cap ~~death by burning.~~

The Victoria Cross has also been awarded to Private Alfred Potts of the 1st ~~Berkshire Yeomanry~~ for most conspicuous bravery and devotion to a wounded comrade in Gallipoli during the fighting on August 21, at the time of the attack on hill seventy. Although he had been himself severely wounded in the thigh, he remained out for over forty-eight hours under the Turkish trenches with another private of his regiment who was severely wounded and unable to move, although he could have himself returned in safety.

Finally he fixed a shovel to the equipment of his wounded comrade and, using this as a sledge, dragged him back over six hundred yards to our lines under the Turkish fire.

Some days we had to lie low while the battleships in the bay dropped a few shells on the Turks. Their aim was marvellous; they repeatedly knocked in Jacko's trenches.

We also had an occasional laugh when we heard the Turkish shells going over our heads and dropping on Chocolate Hill where our regiment was in comparative safety. Unfortunately we were dirtier than we need be, owing to the fact that we had been ordered to leave our 'packs' on the beach when we moved up.

We only had our haversacks and water bottles with us and as the nights were rather chilly, could have done with our greatcoats. Imagine us all this time without a coat, blanket, towel, soap, razor and all the other little things which civilisation brings, then you will realise what a sight we were and how we felt.

On the Friday night we were wakened by Jack Goodson who was sentry. We 'stood-to' at once for firing was breaking out on all sides – we thought a night attack by the Turks had commenced.

For about an hour the firing was fast and furious on both sides, although we could not see a thing except the dim outline of the Turks trenches and the little darts of flame as they fired.

It died down at last. We heard after, that a party of the 'Skins' had been across to 'Jacko's' and dropped a few bombs amongst them, hence the outburst.

It was uncanny, the Turkish fire seemed pretty good, but we had no casualties in our part of the trench even though bullets were flying about in their hundreds.

We were in this position for a week, and then were relieved by the Berkshire MG Section.

The same old struggle was experienced, scrabbling down the trenches again, this time in the middle of the night when most of the men were trying to get some sleep. It took about 2 hours to do a mile of trench.

The following day we spent sleeping and improvising dug-outs. Chocolate Hill had become a favourite spot for the Turkish guns.

On the previous Saturday when we were laughing at the shells going over our heads, our own regiment was catching it severely and although in dug-outs on the side of the hill, there were 67 men hit. Eddie Blackham (a school friend) was killed in this bombardment. 38 Worcester's were put out of use including Bert O'Neill, Walter French and others. Harry Scudder had a narrow escape, his helmet; tunic and haversack were torn to pieces by shrapnel. Luckily we had a 'mail' to cheer us up about this time.

I was very bucked to receive a parcel of 200 cigarettes from pals in the Survey branch of the GPO which was an absolute God-send and very much appreciated by the Gun Sec'n who all participated.

I also had a parcel from home with three beautiful cotton shirts originally intended for wear in Alexandria when going 'down-town'. I put one on, Cyril another and Harry Scudder the third.

We were soon cheered to the echo by the inhabitants of the neighbouring 'burrows' who asked if we had just 'come out'! We sang:

> *'As we walked along the Bois de Boulogne*
> *with an independent air, you could hear the*
> *girls declare "why he's a millionaire" it's the*
> *man who broke the Bank of Monte Carlo'*

1st September 1915: Back again with the Enniskillen's in the trenches and we had another horrible, dull, dirty stretch with not a lot of rest – plenty of hard digging etc.

On the Thursday night (2nd) we were ordered to post double sentries which meant Doug Lamb and Bylie being on sentry all night long.

I thought this was a bit thick, so about midnight I told them to get **down whilst I did a turn myself, but I had overestimated my power and fell asleep standing up and was awakened by an Irish Officer** who was doing the 'rounds' (I discovered afterwards that he had reported me). Here, with my rifle I walked to the edge of the trench and I carefully chose my target and 'sniped' my first Turkish soldier at 700 yards distance from where I aimed.

3rd September 1915: Shelling by the Turks in which Lieutenant Smith, MG Officer of the Enniskillen's with whom I had had several interesting conversations, was killed in his dug-out.

4th September 1915: Very quiet day. Packed up again about 6.00 pm and trekked back to Chocolate Hill.

We were in the open dodging the snipers rather than endure the nightmare of struggling down the trench again. Arrived at 7.00pm and found the regiment ready to move off. Hung about till 11.00 pm when we trekked off to the right to a line of trenches about a mile away (occupied by the 10th Irish Division).

Here we relieved the MG Section of the 7th Dublin Fusiliers, mostly young fellows from Dublin University.

While they were getting their guns off the parapet, someone accidentally pressed the trigger and shot their gunner who was on top in front of the muzzle. The poor chap was killed instantly – we buried him the next day.

We found our new trench much better than the old one and much happier being with our own regiment.

The regiment stayed in this position from 5th Sept to 10th Oct, although I did not last that long due to my Court Martial. Life was very uneventful except for my Court Martial which aroused much interest throughout the Brigade.

It is difficult to reproduce the atmosphere of Gallipoli to anyone who was not there.

I am afraid my position as a prisoner charged with 'sleeping on guard and endangering the life of his comrades' looks very black against me when regarded from a comfortable chair in England.

I can only say that given the same set of circumstances, the same hopeless feeling and the same dead tired comrades, I would do exactly as I did.

Let a man who has been through the 'hell of the trenches' judge me and I know what his verdict will be.

My trial took place in a dug-out with Officers from our own Brigade to try me, with Major Hugh Cheape as President.

Colonel Coventry was good to me and gave me a 'good character' which carried a lot of weight. I was reduced to Private, but felt that I had the Court's sympathy.

Sometime afterwards, Jack Garside told me that on the day of my trial, a Brigade burial grave was marked out and a grave dug which he quite thought was for me (Where Grave is thy Victory?). Harry Scudder verified this.

Our new trench ran from Chocolate Hill on the left to the Sari Bair hills on the right – where the Anzacs were worrying the Turks.

In front of us about 2 miles distant, was the village of Anafarta, which looked very pretty especially in the evening, with its Mosque and thin pointed Minaret standing high above the little white houses.

It was near this village that the remains of about 100 Norfolk men were found five years after they were killed. This company consisted mostly of Territorials from Sandringham on the King's estate. They went astray during a night attack on the 12th August and were never seen again – there were no survivors.

Another beautiful view that I recollect was at sunset. From our position in the trenches we could look west towards the Aegean Sea, the Isle of Samothrace was the nearest to us and the evening sun behind the island was a sight to behold.

We soon had some pretty comfortable dug-outs in our new positions, the digging was easy, and no rocks as we'd had on the hills.

My chum in this position was Bylevelt who was a real good'un and furthermore he was a good cook! Our rations were still biscuits (I never tasted bread on the peninsula), Bully, one small piece of bacon per day, dried fruit (figs and apricots) and jam.

I shall never forget the latter, apricot being a novelty for us. But day after day still eating apricot, we all got heartily sick of the stuff.

The rations were enough to live on, but no surplus and what was worse, no variety.

I forgot to note that we had dried vegetables in tins occasionally, but these required a tremendous lot of soaking and as we all suffered from tender stomachs, due no doubt to the rough conditions and quantity of dirt that we ate, anything that was not easily digested soon upset us.

Luckily the Engineers dug a well nearby so that we did not have to go far to fetch water, but it was still rationed as water was very scarce on the peninsula.

The Navy fetched some from Alexandria in petrol cans. Our chief problem was firewood; we had many a risky try into 'no-man's land' for brushwood as the ground behind the trenches was soon cleared up, there were one or two small trees.

I remember one where "D" Squadron was situated and some of us used to sit under it for a bit of shade.

There was a dead man's boot projecting from his grave in the middle of the group, this came in very handy for knocking one's pipe on – we were quite hardened to little details like that.

Our only trouble was with the Turks sniping which was indulged in by both sides. We could hold our own by now and often put Jacko's snipers out of business.

Fred March of 'A' Squadron did very well; he collected quite a number of scalps. We also did a lot of 'sapping' (digging a trench forward towards the enemy) but I am glad to say that we MG men were excused this job.

Coventry Sap and Hugh Sap were the Worcester's masterpieces. We had one or two night alarms which are very annoying to say the least, especially if it is your turn for a nap, and of course, the everlasting 'stand to' at 4.00 am every morning.

We now had our greatcoats, one blanket each and our packs brought up from the beach, these were very welcome as the nights were awfully cold.

On Saturday 11th September, just as we had the 'Billies' going, the Turks opened up a terrific bombardment and rifle fire on our trench.

We all thought that we were in for a scrap; we had to leave our grub and hop up on the parapet to meet Jacko if he came. We returned his fire as well as we could.

After half an hour blazing away at each other, the row died down. Tysoe and George Smith had got a little piece of steak from rations (we had a little fresh meat now and then). They had it nicely cooked when the row started. Being loathe to leave it for a few nasty Turks, they carried on with their meal.

I shall not forget the way Lieutenant Colville danced around when he found them. We had a few casualties this afternoon, Brigadier-General Wiggin was wounded and Mann (Lieutenant Haynes' batman) was killed.

Trench life began to get on our nerves; we had to get up to all sorts of games to keep ourselves going for it was a hopeless existence. I do not write much of fighting, but let me hasten my reader to explain that we took our lives in our hands all day long.

If you peep over the parapet you would draw a bullet almost at once, believe me, life was never easy!

One task that was always dangerous was the fetching of rations and water. As you went along the trench, every corner you turned became a death trap.

There were spots where everyone from Generals down had to 'duck and run'. We had casualties every day.

Sickness began to make inroads into our strength, every man that left us made more work for those who remained.

Digging had to be continued, sentries, look outs, snipers, fatigue parties and wiring parties etc went on just the same.

Instead of it being your turn, say 1 in 4, it gradually increased until it became 1 in 2 or a perpetual grind.

Jack Goodson was our first sick man. He fell ill with fever and filed away to the beach.

I later heard from him that he went straight on to the Aquitania and was in "Blighty" in five days – some luck that! George Field followed, he had dysentery and went to Malta, and Phillip Everitt was next and was shipped to Egypt.

Shorty (Harold Wood) fell ill with jaundice and was taken off. My turn soon came; I had a horrible attack of dysentery (Typhoid).

I fought against it for 5 days and never left my dug-out, but eventually had to give in, feeling more dead than alive. I am sure I should never have made it (2½ miles) to the hospital on the beach if it had not been for my good friend George Smith who half carried me there.

After going before a Doctor and having a label stuck on, I went on board a barge with about 20 other men all like myself, too weak to stand. We were towed out to the hospital ship "Neuralia" which was lying about a mile from the beach.

The first thing we did was to go below and get into a warm bath. I stripped and pushed all my clothes through a port-hole to make sure I should never wear them again, for after six weeks in those filthy trenches everyone was covered with vermin.

An Orderly gave me a suit of pyjamas and I was soon between some beautiful white sheets which seemed to me as near to heaven as I had ever been before - so ended my stay on that slaughter ground, Gallipoli.

It is some years since I was there, but its memory will never fade.

I shall always remember the hopeless dawns, the thirst, hunger, filth, heat, stench and the millions of great green flies coming off the unburied corpses and settling on one's food, the sunken cheeks and staring eyes of men dying.

It was a ghastly hole and I ought to thank God every day that he brought me safely through it all and back to England, Home and Beauty.

We had many rough times afterwards on the desert and in the hills of Palestine, but they were not to be compared with Gallipoli.

Chapter 11

Farewell to Gallipoli: 1915

We steamed away on the Neuralia on the 23rd September, put into Lemnos Harbour for a few hours and then on to Alexandria.

I don't remember much about the voyage, I only saw the Doctor once. He just poked his head into the cabin where four of us were lying and asked if we were alright.

Doctors and Nurses worked like Trojans on these ships, for they were packed full with sick and wounded, every deck and gangway filled with men, some half dead.

Deaths were numerous; there was no funeral service just a blanket sewn round the body and down the plank to the sea.

At Alexandria I was taken to the government hospital, a permanent hospital with civilian Doctors and native staff. They looked after me very well, so I recovered rapidly.

I was there about three weeks and was then discharged, feeling far from well, but men were coming in every day in their hundreds from the peninsula.

There was no time to bother with people who could stand on their own legs! Luckily the hospital was quite near our old camp at Chatby, so I just toddled down there and was soon amongst the friends whom we left behind with the horses.

They were all very glad to have any of the lads back who had been "over there" and were very keen to hear the news of our 'doings'.

The latest news they could tell me was that the regiment mustered only 70 men, this shows the wastage caused by sickness and casualties – our strength when we left Egypt for Gallipoli was about 350. Whilst at Chatby, I paid a visit to Mr Toy at Ibrahimich and had two jolly 'English' evenings with him and his family.

Also at Chatby I heard that Bylevelt and Austin Woodward followed me over, so we went to their hospital to see them. Bylie looked terribly ill.

28th October 1915: We packed up everything at Chatby and with the help of some natives (engaged for the purpose), moved camp to Mena, near Cairo.

This was a fearful ordeal for there were about 400 horses and only about 50 of us. The Egyptians were triers but had no idea, and as everyone had three or four horses, we had our hands full.

However, we arrived at Mena Camp eventually and found ourselves right up against the Pyramids on the ground that the Anzacs had vacated when they went to Gallipoli a few months previously. Our first night here was rather upset by shouts at about 3.00 am. We tumbled out and found that the Nile flood had risen right up to our camp and had flooded the cook-house and QM stores – luckily this was the highest that it reached or we should have had all our belongings soaked!

Mena is about 10 miles from the Nile, but every year in October the overflow spreads all over the surrounding countryside, which consequently is made fertile. One can tell to a few yards how far the flood water reaches because the dark rich soil ceases and the yellow sands begin. Unfortunately for us, this particular year it happened to be an unusually high flood, hence our discomfiture. I was not feeling at all well at this period, in fact I had not recovered fully from the previous illness. I gradually became worse again until one morning I went to Dr Bullock of the Warwick's with a temperature and was sent off to Mena House Hotel, which was being used as a hospital.

I had a bad week as my complaint could not apparently be diagnosed. It was eventually decided that I had enteric fever and I was put in a motor van and sent to Choubra Hospital, near Cairo Station. Choubra Hospital, formerly an Austrian Hospital, was very clean and cool. I spent nearly two months here and thoroughly enjoyed it after the first 2-3 weeks.

During this time I lived mostly on liquids eventually progressing to a chicken diet until Christmas Day when I was allowed to sit down to turkey and a small piece of pudding!

Whilst at Choubra I received a letter from Cyril Coombs on Gallipoli. He told me that Tysoe had got himself transferred to the Australians to be with his brother, in spite of strenuous opposition from Lieutenant Colville. Pikey Adams had been invalided off with dysentery and George Smith with a scalded foot and septic sores. That just left Kemp (now Sergeant), Cyril (now Corporal), Doug Lamb, Hewins, Wright and Jack Middleton.

9th December 1915: An orderly at the hospital informed me that the Yeomanry Division had at last arrived at Mena from Suvla Bay. This news bucked me up for I now knew that it would not be long before I saw my old pals again. I did not have long to wait, for the very next day I was fetched downstairs and found dear old Cyril, with a smile across his face, looking fat and well. He told me all that had happened since I left them.

Doug Lamb wounded in the arm, Hewins, 'Middy' and Wright invalided off. Out of the original machine gun section of 15 men, only Kemp and Cyril came back the normal way, with the regiment. Towards Christmas I recovered my legs and managed to get a pass or two with Sergeant Pulzer of the City of London Yeomanry (the Sharpshooters). It was on one of these passes that I last saw my best pal Cyril Coombs, we spent the afternoon in Cairo Zoo (a beautifully laid out park), and finished up with supper in the Obelisk Café near the Kursaal.

Cyril left us at the café to beg a lift the 10 miles to Mena – I believe he was Corporal of the Guard or something similar. His cheery smile seemed sad to me, because I had a good idea that I might soon be on a ship for Blighty. Cyril was killed at Katia four months later.

The Nurses excelled themselves at Christmas, which all combined to give us a jolly good time – which we certainly had, finishing up with a concert. We were all given a Christmas present which, we were told, came from British residents in Cairo. My present was a Brass Bowl with Arabic inscriptions which I managed to bring home.

24B - Brass bowl given to me as a gift from the British residents of Cairo to the invalids in Choubra Hospital Christmas 1915

As it was a hospital for infectious diseases, we were barred from having visitors, which was a good thing, especially for stomach troubles. One thing that struck me very forcibly while in this hospital was the beautiful climate of the country. We had our Christmas dinner in pyjamas and could sit out on the flat roof, dressed in this light fashion at any time of the day - we invalids, too!!

28th December 1915: The Doctor came round the ward and asked most of us if we thought we were well enough to take a long voyage to a nasty cold country! If we preferred it, we could have a trip up the Nile to Luxor, which was a place where millionaires spent the winter in peace time.

One strange fellow out of about 30, chose Luxor (I think he must have had a nagging wife at home). The rest plumped for the cold country called Blighty (England).

We drew our kit the same night and left the next morning by train to Alexandria where we boarded a hospital ship (the "Lanfranc") and sailed at 4.00 pm on 29th December 1915.

I have warm recollections of my time at Choubra Hospital. As I said before it was an infectious disease hospital and visitors were not allowed (Cyril Coombs got in by bribery and corruption!), so we had to make our own amusements.

Dr Rankin, Sisters Godden, Law and Eddie, Orderlies Owen (Middlesex Yeomanry), Saunders (Dorsets), Jones (Gloucester's) all helped to make our stay pleasant.

The "Lanfranc" was a nice ship belonging to the Booth Line. We had a comfortable trip, much different to the journey out in the Saturnia. Pulzer, Jackson, Pearson and I passed the time away at Auction Bridge, which we commenced at Choubra and continued for four months.

Chapter 12
Homeward Bound recovery from Typhoid

1st January 1916: We passed close to Malta but did not stop.

5th January 1916: Anchored in Gibraltar Harbour – we were not allowed ashore, so contented ourselves with buying fruit etc from the hawkers who swarmed round the ship in small boats. "How much are the oranges, Antonio?" "Orrite, never mind, put ze money in ze basket".

9th January 1916: Arrived in Spithead on a typical cold, foggy morning after 2-3 days rough passage through the 'Bay'. Everybody on tip-toe anxious to get ashore, but the Britannic got into Southampton first and filled all the available trains, so we had to wait on board till the following day when we entrained and were carried up to Whalley Hospital near Blackburn.
We had half an hour at Snow Hill Station, Birmingham for tea.
I had no opportunity of letting anyone know that I was in England as I saw nobody that I knew. It was dark when we reached Whalley, but next morning we found we were in a very large hospital, situated on high ground with a grand view all round.

26 - Morning exercise by the Auction Bridge Four All from different regiments making a good recovery from their ordeal at Gallipoli

I was now pretty strong and able to get about. I paid several visits to Blackburn, Clitheroe, Accrington, Stoneyhurst College and other places in the neighbourhood. Time went quickly here, nine weeks slipped by and I was at last discharged.

17th March 1916: 6 weeks leave – arriving home and visiting pre-War haunts and friends. I learnt that many of my old pals had joined the Army, many of them in City Battalions of the

Warwickshire Regiment (conscription had not been introduced yet). I also visited my pre-War department in Birmingham GPO and was warmly greeted by the lucky men who had been refused by all Services owing to physical defects.

After these experiences, I was glad to return to the company of my friends who were serving, and I reported in due course to Regimental Headquarters at Worcester.

I was taken from there, with others, to Malvern where a 'convalescent home' had been established in the pre-War headquarters of the Malvern Squadron. The only Officer concerned was an old Major who owned a carpet factory at Kidderminster.

He visited us about once a fortnight, but as his factory was busy, he could not spare much time for regimental duties (although he was drawing Army pay).

The senior NCO was Sergeant Major Jack Downes who lived on the premises (see the start of this book). We had a visit by a local Sergeant Major Underhill two or three times a week.

He did not drill us but took us on country walks for exercise. We also had a few visits to Malvern Rifle Range.

Whilst at Malvern, as we were settling down to our comfortable quarters, we read in the papers that our regiment had suffered terrible disasters at Oghratina and Katia on the Sinai Desert.

This occurred on Easter Sunday 23rd April 1916. More than 100 of our old comrades had been 'killed in action'.

This put a heavy shadow on our life at Malvern and most of us were anxious to go out again to avenge our old pals. Our move didn't come until October, probably due to the shortage of transport.

We were sent to Tidworth Barracks on Salisbury Plain. The barracks were fully occupied by recruits and convalescents of the Dragoon Guards.

Canvas tents with wooden floors were provided for Yeomanry – this was satisfactory for a month or so, but with frost coming on in early November, shaving with an Army razor was difficult in ice cold water. We were mixed with recruits and were expected to participate in the recruit training – much undignified for veterans of Gallipoli!

We lived in winter conditions at Tidworth for a few more weeks but in December we were warned that we should soon be moving.

We also learnt that due to a shortage of transport and torpedoing by the enemy, we were to travel by train across France to Marseilles, from where we would be transported by a French ship.

28 - On a country walk at Malvern

Chapter 13

My second trip out East

Our party had a good send-off, the Dragoons played us all the way through the Barracks to lively tunes, which made you feel 'what a fine thing it was to be a soldier going abroad to fight'.

Sid Cranch, Billy Cruse and other old pals came to the station to see us off and were sorry that they were not coming with us.

After a short railway journey we reached Southampton where we hung about on the Docks until nightfall when we went aboard one of the little Cross Channel steamers which took British troops to France. We were packed on this boat as if we were a lot of refugees on the last ship leaving! As every man on board had about 60lbs of kit with Arms and Equipment, you can imagine what a crowd there was. Lights of all kinds were strictly forbidden.

There was nothing for it but to scrape a place for yourself amongst the kit and lie down for a sleep. It would have been all over with us if a submarine had nipped us, but we felt safe in the thought that thousands of troops had gone across in the same way without any accidents. The sailors told us that there were look-out ships about every half mile right across the Channel when troops were moving, so it would have been impossible for a submarine to evade the watch as the History of the War has proved.

After an uncomfortable night, we arrived in France at daybreak. It was cold, wet and dirty and not at all 'La Belle France'.

We marched through the town, about three miles to a large camp on the cliffs, a very tiring march as we had to carry all our kit.

I was lucky enough to enlist the services of a small French boy to carry my bags. The camp was a morass of mud, but we were put into tents with wooden floorboards, so were able to keep fairly dry.

Our first aim was to get some food and after a search we found an Army canteen. This was the first affair of the kind I had seen. I was surprised at the sensible way it was administered.

We had similar canteens out east and they were fine institutions which did much more good for the troops than any other institute. The prices were always the lowest, the food supplied always the best and we felt very grateful to the originators of the NACB.

Ste Andresse Camp was surrounded with barbed wire, but Harry Scudder, Windram and I managed to get out and go down town for a look round. Le Havre has some very fine streets and one or two large squares, but also had some dirty slums down by the docks. On our march through the town we were interested to see large gangs of German and Austrian prisoners at work.

13th December 1916: Left the camp at about 3.00 pm and marched down the hill to the station where we entrained in the usual French carriages (hard seats and straight backs). In my carriage were Skudder, Binstead and Windram, not a bad little party for the two day journey. We played Solo nearly the whole time.

The train left at 8.30 pm, stopped at Yvetot and Rouen. This appeared a very large city and we were surprised to see the lights all blazing in contrast to the darkened English cities we had left.

The journey through the night was very slow with frequent stops, due no doubt to the congested state of the line.

We arrived at Versailles at 5.00 am on the 14th December and were met by a party of ladies of the Croix Rouge who distributed coffee and cakes – most enjoyable. Our next stop was Juvissy, a small town where I managed to buy some bread and Camembert cheese for our party.

From here we followed the River Seine through Melins, Champagne-sur-Seine, along the Yonne valley through Sens (a fine old Cathedral town) to Laroche, Department of Yonne.

We had a halt here for 1½ hours and managed to get a good wash and a hot meal. Passing through several small towns, we reached Dijon at 10.00 pm. Dijon is the centre of the wine district.

It is also famous for the extraordinary run of luck that Binstead had with the cards while we were stuck in the long railway tunnel at the approach to the town.

Lyons was reached at 6.00 am on the 15th December. I was sorry that we did not see much of this fine city on the River Rhone, but I saw it again on my return home. Skudder, I recollect, was interested in Lyons.

As day broke, we proceeded on our journey south and we reached beautiful country. The line ran alongside the Rhone for miles and we could see the Cevennes Mountains away to the west and the beginning of the Alps to the East.

These foothills rose straight from the railway and were covered with vineyards, an impressive landscape. We halted at Valence at 10.30 am and a few of us dashed out of the station for some bread and wine etc for the benefit of the party.

We could now see the high Alps in the distance, about 30 miles away I would estimate. They looked very fine with their tops covered with snow. Our next stop was Orange, not a picturesque little place as its name signifies, but rather nasty and dirty. However, we did have some nice coffee and rum, so I will not libel the place!

Avignon, the ancient capital of Provence, was reached at 3.00 pm. From the railway the old City looked full of interesting old buildings, castles and Churches.

I thought what a good place it would be for a quiet holiday after the War. We passed Tarascon, just as the sun was setting, which gave a deep red glow to the old houses of this ancient town.

Arles was reached around 5.30 pm and we had a few minutes' halt during which time we stretched our legs.

Towards 9.00 pm we ran through a very long tunnel (approx 2 miles). Eventually we drew up at our destination, Marseilles, after a very interesting journey in spite of the uncomfortable carriage in which we had 'lived' in for two days and nights. We marched from the Docks station to the Rest Camp at Carcassonne which was situated in a little ravine with huge fences all round. It resembled a Prisoner of War compound!

16th December 1916: We rose from our blankets to find we were in a nice looking little camp with the sea in the near distance. During the day we were taken down to the Docks for fatigues and it did not take a lot of dodging to get away from the work and into a snug little café. I was surprised to see the different nationalities of soldiers we met at Marseilles. English Tommies, French Poilus, Indians of our Army, Negroes of the French Senegalese, French Chinamen from Cochin China with funny shaped hats.
We had quite an interesting outing and got back to the docks in time to march back to camp with the gallant lads who had been working hard all day.

17th December 1916: Spent a quiet day in camp with an evening at the ancient game of "Housey Housey".

18th December 1916: It was a wet day and the camp soon churned up into thin mud, which was not nice to sleep on.
After Harry and I helped a stall holder carry her stores out of the camp, we got clear for an evening. We boarded a tram at St. Louis and spent a few hours in the great wicked city.
I was surprised at the distance we were out, two or three miles right round the harbour. Marseilles impressed me. It has some very fine main streets and boulevards. Although it was December, it was quite warm without our coats, even sitting outside drinking a modest "Café et Cognac".
Our evening was very crowded for we knew that we would soon be sailing for Egypt. In fact this proved to be our one and only visit to the city. Before we caught the tram to St. Louis, we had a look round the demi-mondaine quarter and found to our surprise that Marseilles was every bit as bad as Alexandria for brazen immorality.
It made us feel quite sick to see Negroes going about with white women. However, this is the black side of Marseilles and I am pleased to say that it has a brighter side also. It is a wonderful city, set in a beautiful situation.
It has a large harbour within easy reach of resorts on the Mediterranean, where it is summer all year round. I hope to see Marseilles again before I die.

19th December 1916: Quiet day in camp. We heard that we were to continue our long journey the following day. Harry and I got out again and had a real French supper in the house of Madame, a widow whose husband had been killed at Verdun.

Mrs. Moore and Madam Jourdain were very good friends to us at Marseilles. Unfortunately we had spent a lot of money on our long train journey, so we could not reciprocate as we should have wished.

Chapter 14

On board the Liner Kalyan from Marseilles

20th December 1916: Sailed from Marseilles at sunset in the PO liner Kalyan, escorted by a TBD 57. We sailed between Italy and Sardinia. The latter, barely 5 miles away seemed to be a huge country with tremendous mountains covered with snow. It appeared more impressive because the mountains seemed to rise straight from the sea. Steaming along the coast of Sardinia and at around 10.00 pm I fell asleep. We didn't see anything of Malta but observed that the TBD 57 was replaced by the D2 (Destroyer) which pointed to the fact that we were near a naval base.

We noticed our course had changed from SE to about NNE which mystified us. But we discovered the reason we were zig-zagging amongst the islands of the Grecian Archipelago, was to avoid submarines. During the day a patrol boat joined our escort and it appeared that we were sailing round one small island with the idea of waiting until dark. At sunset, we went full speed ahead for Egypt and the following morning the Isles of Greece were not visible.

25th December (Christmas Day) 1916: During the morning we took part in many different sports and had a concert in the afternoon. Sandover boxed in an exhibition bout and did well.

We then spent a miserable evening below deck playing cards, without a drink or a smoke. We rolled ourselves up in our blankets at an early hour and were lulled to sleep by the sound of our Officers keeping up Christmas in the approved way – there seemed to be no lack of drinks in the saloon judging by the corks popping!

No. 13 Draft embarked at Southampton 11th December 1916, crossed France to Marseilles by train, embarked again on the 20th December and arrived in Alexandria 26th December. This was the largest Draft ever sent to the regiment, consisting of one Officer and 120 other ranks. 30 of them were men who had been invalided home after Gallipoli. This draft brought the regiment up to strength for the first time since the disaster at Oghratina and Katia in April 1916.

26th December (Boxing Day) 1916: We arrived in Alexandria Harbour at about 11.00 am, disembarked and marched to Ramleh train terminus (memories of a similar march in 1915). We boarded the well remembered old train, passed Chatby Camp and arrived at Mustapha (Sidi Gaber station).

27th December 1916: Tea with Mrs Toy at Ibrahimieh – I cabled home.

28th December 1916: Dinner at Mrs Toy's plus a real good evening

29th December 1916: Went down town with Skudder, Binstead, Windram and met Sid Filkins and Frank Davies. We visited a few of the old cafes where we had spent happy times with Cyril Coombes, Eddie Blackham and others of the old regiment who left England in the old days but were, alas, sleeping the long sleep. The evening brought back many sad recollections to those of us who had been here before.

30th December 1916: We left Mustapha about 10.00 pm and entrained at Sidi Gaber station. On the way, our pantomime Officer, distinguished himself by shouting to a sleepy old Arab "Yalla Imshi Station" (this was of course to air his knowledge of Arabic) it meant "go away, get out, station".
We old hands had a good laugh at him. Sergeant Morris turned up rather the worse for wear at the station. As he was rather noisy "Cinema Joe" said he would be placed under arrest. Morris, however, was sober enough to know a thing or two and immediately said that if he was under arrest, he was not allowed to carry arms or ammunition and dumped down his rifle and equipment forthwith.

This put our fool of a leader in a quandary because everybody had more to carry than they comfortably could, so he ordered Morris' release. We arrived at Kantara early in the morning and marched across the Suez Canal to the camp for our regimental details. We found a comfortable little camp on the sand with a good Mess. Lawson Kemp, Alf Dawes, Percy Hawkes and several other old friends met us and we were soon at home asking questions about their activities since we left them on Gallipoli.

As it was New Year's Eve when we arrived, we had to 'let the New Year in' properly, which was done in the usual style.

Chapter 15

1917 Return to Sinai Desert

After resting for two days at Kantara, we entrained on the new railway which had been built across the desert. We had to clamber up on the top of loaded goods trucks. This railway line is a wonderful piece of work, but has not received the notice it deserves in the "Home Press". It was laid down at the rate of a mile a day on the sands of the Sinai Desert. The rough work carried out by Egyptian natives and the engineering by English RE soldiers. Along this line, all supplies were taken for the large Army that finally smashed the Turks in Palestine. Parallel to the railway, a water main was laid for over 100 miles to bring fresh water to the troops. Every few miles, little concrete stations were erected, which served as bases for parties of Royal Engineers and native Egyptians whose job it was to keep the railway and water lines open.

This is not such a simple affair as it sounds because the sand is continually blowing on to the line and covering it up. If it is not cleared immediately a derailed train could result.

The journey across the limitless desert is very interesting at first, but one soon tires of miles and miles of yellow sand and longs for a break in the monotony such as the little green hills of England.

It is now possible to do the journey in a sleeping car. The stations on the new line used to be Gilban, Pelusium, Katia, Romani, Bir Ed Abd, Tilul, Mazar, Maadu and El Arish.

The wooden cross at Ogratina Hill, where our regiment fought to the end, was visible from the line, but I heard afterwards that the wind had moved the cross and most of the hill. After an all day journey (during which we passed Katia where our regiment was cut up about nine months ago), we arrived at railhead Kilo 139 at 11.00 pm in pouring rain and pitch darkness.

Luckily we dropped across the regimental dump at the railhead with Billy Shillon in charge. Billy tumbled out of his shack and soon had an acceptable "Dixie" of tea for us. Captain Noel Pearson (the Adjutant) and Jack Brodie RSM, rode up shortly afterwards and gave us a welcome which warmed our hearts, as the tea did our stomachs.

4th January 1917: At daybreak the horses arrived and we rode across the sand to the regiment (living in little shacks made out of palm leaves, in bivouacs at El Bitia, two miles from the railway). The boys crowded us and gave us a good welcome – which did us good. They looked a thoroughly disreputable lot to us, who had come straight from the land of clean buttons.

There were only 50 left of the original regiment, including 23 who had not been home since April 1915.

We settled in and after one night at El Bitia, we marched to El Arish, from where the Turks had just evacuated. I should mention here that on our allocation to squadrons on our arrival, I asked to be excused the machine gun section and was placed with"D" Squadron with whom I remained for the rest of the War.

I am pleased to say that I never regretted this move but wished I had been with 'D' all the way through. The Officers were nearly all new faces to me, Lieutenant Colonel H. J. Williams of the 1st Kings Dragoons was O/C, Major Ian Straker of the 9th Lancers in charge of "D" Squadron, Major Ffrench-Blake MC of the 21st Lancers "A" Squadron and our own Major 'Bill' Wiggin with "C" Squadron (in addition, 20 junior officers to replace the losses at Katia).

Our march to El Arish was very interesting to me as this was my first taste of desert soldiering, like all new experiences they fascinate to a certain degree.

I was astounded at the height of some of the sand hills (200 and 300 foot hills were common). The hills were constantly changing as the sand is blown by the wind from one hill and forms another some distance away.

The common idea of the desert being one level stretch of sand is entirely wrong, as there are hills and valleys everywhere.

On the desert we had to do all our marching by compass bearings by day and the stars by night. When we had to make a long detour to get round a big hill it made our bearings difficult to adhere to. The going was terrible for the horses as the poor beasts always went in over the fetlocks, frequently as deep as their knees and hocks. It had the same effect on men, everybody walked with a long, slow stride, like the plough-boy at home.

In fact when we went down to Cairo for a few days leave, we all suffered with stiff legs and backs due to walking on the hard pavements!

Chapter 16

El Arish (oasis, figs, dates) 100 miles from Suez

After three days at El Arish, we had orders to saddle up as lightly as possible and moved off with the Desert Mounted Corps at 4.00 pm to attack the Turks at Rafa, 25 miles away.

Our regiment was an advance guard to the Corps and 'D' was the leading squadron. So here I was, in Egypt a fortnight, going into action right up in the first line. I thought to myself more than once, "Godrich, you fool, why didn't you stop at Malvern a bit longer?"

We pushed ahead right through the night across an unknown desert where English troops had never been before.

Luckily we struck nothing worse than a few Bedouins looking very frightened – also several jackals. A halt was made at last at an Arab village called Sheik Zoaid, close to a large lake. We were now about four miles from the hill named El Magruntin on which the Turks were entrenched – we were to attack at dawn!

28B - E V Godrich at his bivouack in El Arish, Sword in sand

There was one little preliminary in which our regiment was interested, it was a Turkish patrol of about 12 men on camels which was said to come out for a look around the country just before dawn. It was our job to capture this patrol, if possible without firing. We were placed out in small parties right across the front and spent several hours in bitterly cold winds which made our teeth chatter, waiting for the enemy patrol which never came.

Just before dawn we saw some wagons approaching which turned out to be our own Brigade Hospital.

This party had somehow lost their way and marched right through our lines straight towards the Turks. Instead of letting them march right into their hands, the Turks opened fire on them so the drivers turned round and came quietly back to us. This was rather an anti-climax for us after our freezing night on the look-out.

9th January 1917: As soon as dawn broke, the firing commenced. The Turkish outposts soon caught sight of us. During the night the Australian horses had made a big detour and had gone right round to the back of the enemy position – we now had them surrounded.

It looked a formidable job as it was a large flat hill that commanded the country for miles. They could see every move we made and they seemed to be very strong in numbers (judging by the firing). Fortunately the HAC Battery had come with us across the desert. These boys opened fire on the position with great effect – they hammered the Turkish trenches well for about an hour, then ceased fire and a Brigade of Australians galloped up to about 1000 yards distance from the Turks and dismounted (apparently with the idea of rushing the position). However, Jacko was not beaten yet and we soon saw men and horses falling in all directions. Their leader saw their mistake, mounted and galloped quickly away.

The Artillery opened up again and we all advanced to within firing distance. We left our horses under cover and took our place with the line of men on foot – now advancing on the hill from all sides.

The Turks gave us a very warm reception; they could hardly do anything else, for they could not run away even had they wanted to. The line in advance of our regiment (and the Warwick's) was quite open, without a scrap of cover. Several machine guns were trained on us. We listened for the MGs then dropped flat whilst the bullets whistled above us – just like a huge scythe going through the air. We jumped up and advanced again.

Jack Brodie, just behind me, was hit in the chest, Clarence Chapman in the thigh and Gus Gibney of the Warwick's (the Brigade humorist) and Springfield of the Gloucester's were both killed. Our regiment suffered 16 wounded but the Warwick's and Gloucester's had greater losses (Warwick's 4 dead, 35 wounded and Gloucester's 5 dead and 38 wounded). Total British casualties were 500 (mostly light wounds).

The position was carried at dusk with 3,000 prisoners; we then had a 25 mile March home. We watered the horses at Sheik Zouid, their first drink for 36 hours. I shall never forget that march – a gruelling day, preceded by a long march and terribly cold outpost, we had all reached the limit of human endurance.

Practically everybody slept in the saddle and left it to the horse to get them home. The next day we had the Christmas free issue of canteen goods out of profits made by the canteen during the previous 12 months.

Rest camp at El Arish on the shore of the Mediterranean sea

We remained at El Arish for a month. We had a pleasant little bivouac in a fig orchard, relieved at intervals by visits from Taubes dropping bombs – they seemed chiefly interested in the progress of the new railway line.

I heard that the natives working on the line had a number killed. Whilst at El Arish we came into contact with the famous 52nd Division "Jocks". We enjoyed playing football with them but their bagpipes nearly drove us mad!

The C/O organised a map reading competition at El Arish in which I managed to get top marks and was rewarded with a dinky little compass and 30/-. My section was Jack Mills, Reg Fearn, Percy Hodgetts, Bill Lendrum.

A sequel to the Rafa scrap was when it was announced that Bill Walker, our troop Sergeant, had been awarded the DCM.

Ernest Cotterill (our shoeing smith) the MM and Buckman (stretcher bearer) the MM and Sergeant Walker was rewarded for carrying on with the troop after our Officer (Ganner) had turned tail and fled. The only example of cowardice our regiment experienced throughout the War.

The days passed at El Arish – a pretty little place where the Wadi El Arish comes down from the hills inland and empties into the sea. The fig orchards extended for miles.

There is a large plantation of date palms right up to the seashore. We appreciated El Arish much more about eight months later when we came down for a rest during the hot weather.

9th February 1917 : We moved camp up the desert to El Burj – a small cluster of Tamarisk trees on the sand hills, with water in abundance, about 100 yards from the sea.

I found it very mysterious that fresh water could be found by digging so near the Mediterranean, but the fact remains that all the way up the coast good water was found – maybe the sand filtered the water.

We had a lot of rain at El Burj so we had to dig into the sand to make our little bivouacs as weatherproof as possible. My half-section here was Bill Lendrum, a peculiar chap but a good chum. My previous chum was Clarence Chapman who "stopped one" at Rafa and was now in hospital.

Our work at El Burj consisted of patrols and outposts, suffering several nights at the latter – bitterly cold and wet. Nothing exciting happened with the enemy except the capture of stray Turks every other day, some deserting and some patrols whom we galloped down. One of the deserters spoke French and we learned that the enemy was preparing a strong position at El Shouth near the Wadi Ghuzze. We saw this a few weeks later.

Whilst at this camp an inter-troop football competition was played and we also had several games of rugger with neighbouring regiments who kept rolling up. When we first arrived at El Burj we were the advanced regiment and responsible for the protection of the Army at El Arish, ten miles behind us.

The outposts were consequently very arduous, a Lance Corporal and three men frequently sent out into the desert for 6-8 miles with nothing to guide them but their compass and common sense.

It was real cavalry work and we all enjoyed it, especially as extra rations were often arriving by camel transport from El Arish to which the railway had now reached.

22nd February 1917: Once more I set my foot on the ladder of success, for I was made up to Lance Corporal (7 weeks after joining the old mob). In addition, I was packed off to Cairo for a course of Hotchkiss gun training as these were soon to be issued to all cavalry units. My pals on the course were Sergeant Walker, Stan Needham, Alcock, Arthur Palmer, Goodwin and Jack Young. It was an enjoyable little 'holiday' although we were kept at the gun very closely during the daytime.

Our headquarters were at Zeitoun near Heliopolis, just a tram ride out of the city. We spent most of our evenings writing up our notes but managed to get into Cairo two or three times.

On one of these occasions I took Arthur Palmer with me to see Mr Chinn who entertained us to a nice little supper.

7th March 1917: We finished the course and left Cairo to proceed back to El Burj, just in time to move to Sheik Zoaid on 10th March. We camped by the seashore where we had a fearful wind blowing our bivvies over and churning up the sand for 3 or 4 days and nights. We were now in 'reserve' so there were no outposts to do. To save us from getting 'rusty' we were put on sword and rifle drill in the soft sand, which was very tiring.

The results of the course in Cairo were announced as follows: Out of a possible 100 marks: Lieutenant Edwards 98 – Palmer 90 – Godrich 89 – Walker 87 – Needham 82 – Alcock 81. Young didn't stay the distance owing to an accident.

He spent a merry evening in Cairo, got hold of a donkey and galloped the five miles to Seitoun and pulled up outside the Guard tent. He said afterwards, that the Guard arrested him for not saluting properly when mounted (by cutting the right hand smartly down to the side). The Sergeant of the Guard said that he couldn't stand up!

19th March 1917: Our Topees (helmets) arrived for which were very grateful as it had been too warm for caps during the past two weeks.*(See Equipment in Appendix)*

21st March 1917: We moved to Rafa, passing en-route El Magruntein, the scene of the fight on 9th January. We observed several graves of Gloucester Yeomen – buried where they fell.

23rd March 1917: Reconnaissance by the Cavalry Division towards Gaza. We heard rumours that the Turks were evacuating their position at El Shauth so as to be ready for us at Gaza. This reconnaissance was no doubt to prove the truth of the rumours.

Our day's outing was very impressive as we had our first peep of the 'Promised Land'. Rafa is the old frontier between Palestine and Egypt; the Turks fixed this because there is nothing but dry desert south of the frontier, with the exception of El Arish. We all knew by our maps that we were crossing into the Holy Land, but we hardly expected such a transformation that shortly met our gaze. We had been trekking quietly along for some miles and climbed a high ridge. When we topped the ridge the view that met us took our breath away.

Down in the valley laid a large village of white houses surrounded by thousands of trees in bloom, beyond those miles of barley. Everyone was astounded, for it looked the real 'land of milk and honey'. We had arrived in 'time', for March is to Palestine what May is to England.

Memories of a Choir Boy (psalm 65)
The folds shall be full of sheep
The valleys also shall stand
So thick with corn that
They shall laugh and sing

When we reached Palestine in March 1917 there were few sheep, the retreating Turks had taken them, but there were many acres of barley. Gaza barley was in great demand by British distillers and brewers.

29 - Remains of a Church and a Fort (built in the 13th Century)Khan Yunis

The village was Khan Yunis, with a beautiful collection of trees – almonds, oranges, figs, apricots and pomegranate. There is an old building in the village which looked like a Norman castle and looked very incongruous amongst the Arab houses. It is said to be the remains of a building erected by the Crusaders.

We saw Khan Yunis many times – in fact I came through on my way home in March 1919, but it never looked the same as the Army that followed us soon made it a dirty, dusty hole and the railway line was built right through the fruit orchards.

I cannot say whether the reconnaissance was a success. I know the horses enjoyed it for they were eating grass and green barley every moment they could – their first feed of green stuff for many months.

We went as far as a peculiar flat topped hill called Tel el Jemmi, which was a Crusaders stronghold many years ago. This hill is beside a deep watercourse, the Wadi Ghuzze.

Taking the horses to water down Wadi Ghuzzi

We watered our horses, but did not cross it as the Turks held the country the other side. We had only come for a look, not a fight, so we did not push our noses too far. We were glad to get back to our Bivouacs at Rafa for we had a big day at 'Jemmi'. The following day we rested.

29th March 1917: We moved to Deir el Bela, a small Arab village which afterwards became the centre of the Army and a huge railway depot. There was a good supply of water here.

Chapter 17

26th March 1917: First Gaza Battle: We left Deir el Bela at 3.00 am in thick fog (memories of the thick fog that hid the Turks at Katia the previous year). We reached Tel el Jemmi at 7.00 am. The task set was to strike due north through the Turkish line, then to divide, one half facing east towards Beersheba to prevent the Turkish Army from reaching Gaza, the other half of the Cavalry were to advance and envelop Gaza from the east and north, whilst the 53rd Infantry Division attacked the town from the south.

The plan seemed a good one on paper (as explained by our Squadron Leader, Major Ian Straker), unfortunately the thick fog in the morning delayed us and towards the end of the day things went wrong. We spent the greater part of the day on the highest ground we could find waiting for 'Jacko' to put in an appearance.

91

Sergeant Bill Lane took his troop on a little scouting excursion to a spot called Huj; this was where our regiment made a glorious charge 8 months later. 'A' Squadron, under Major Ffrench-Blake, charged a small Turkish camp and discovered and captured 60 Turks – all very comfortable and very surprised to see English troops. Their Commanding Officer had made himself very cosy with a camp bed, sheets, cushions, dressing table and armchair! Our lads took everything that was portable, including two or three chickens.

31 - Tomb of an Arab Sheik

Towards dusk we observed movements a few miles away. Reports began to come in from other outposts that the enemy infantry were coming. We sat tight for half an hour until we could estimate their numbers. When they advanced to about a mile away, we could see that they were in great strength, infantry advancing in open order, line after line.

We were scattered over a wide stretch of country on outposts and we were getting anxious lest our particular post should be forgotten in the withdrawal. We were soon up and away. There had been no need to tell the lads to tighten their girths, for that had already been done. As the bullets began to fly we received the welcome signal to withdraw. We rejoined the Squadron who were already on the move – the rest of the regiment had already moved on. As night closed in we were 'far from home'. We felt, the quicker the better! However, we were soon out of range and settled down to an all night trek back to Jemmi. Our leader Major Straker did not seem very confident of his direction and we were led a very peculiar route. We could tell the direction by the stars and we had 'the wind up' at one time when we noticed that the Major was taking us due north which was straight towards the enemy.

At last we found some armoured cars which pointed us in the right direction, and we found the rest of the regiment and the brigade.

We had a halt for about an hour then mounted and rode off again at 3.00 am.

Apparently, just in time, for day was breaking and as it got light the Turks (who had camped on the ground we vacated earlier) began shelling us. We reached Deir el Bela at 9.00 am.

We sorted the horses and settled down for a sleep when "saddle up" was shouted and after some minutes, cursing everything and everybody, we moved off again to In Seirat (high ground commanding a good view), where we were put on outpost until 5.00 pm. We then withdrew and marched to a small Arab village, Beni Sela, near Khan Yunis where we took up another line of outposts all night.

We had 'bully and biscuits' and waited all morning for the order to mount and move on. At 2.00 pm we went back to Deir Bela. We had a long overdue night's rest – everyone was thoroughly exhausted.

We spent almost three weeks at Deir Bela and as we were close to the sea, took advantage of the bathing facilities. The sun gained in strength every day. It always seemed to be more oppressive in March and April than in the hotter months of the year.

The same can be said in the daily round as the sun at 9.00 am takes more out of you than at noon, probably because the rays strike in a different direction. Whilst at Bela we had scraps of information about our day's work on the 26th – the whole operation was a complete failure, due to the 53rd Division not being able to hold Gaza owing to being out-numbered.

It appeared to be another Suvla Bay affair! Lack of co-operation – the GOC, Sir Archibald Murray directed operations from the Savoy Hotel in Cairo some 200 miles away! The late start due to the fog upset the programme considerably.

The left wing of the cavalry did their part brilliantly. They flanked Gaza, captured a high ridge commanding the town and galloped into Gaza expecting to meet our Infantry – but they were Turks, for the Welsh lads had not get there. This cavalry dash was performed by the New Zealand Mounted Brigade, a fine body of men and horses.

Our total casualties for the day were about 4,000. This was our first reverse and it bucked up the Turks no end. The 53rd Division lost all their camel transport which was captured, and one or two armoured cars also fell into enemy hands.

The 52nd Division (Scots) were kept in reserve at Bela all day and did not fire a shot. We were told that our hurrying to and from different positions for outpost work after the fight was in order, and that we should be ready to meet a counter attack which we thought the Turks would deliver.

2nd April 1917: still at Bela: An event of great importance to me now occurred, the Hotchkiss guns arrived. My life was wrapped up with this gun from this day until the War ended, so I learnt quite a lot about them. The remainder of the week was spent fixing up the new guns, practising loading them on to pack horses, instructing our teams and finally firing them which we did on the beach.

Chapter 18

6th April 1917 (Good Friday): Spent the day at In Seirat digging trenches on a high ridge. It was very hot and dusty and we were all tired and fed up when we returned to our bivouacs.

8th April 1917 (Easter Sunday): Church parade in the morning and firing the guns in the afternoon.

9th April 1917 (Easter Monday): The Hotchkiss guns were paraded with their teams for inspection by our old Brigadier, General Wiggin. This was his last parade for on the following day Colonel Fitzgerald was appointed Brigadier and our old leader returned to Egypt and soon after returned to England.

He was very popular as Brigadiers go, for he had commanded our brigade (Warwick's, Worcester and Gloucester's) since the outbreak of War. He was known to have plenty of pluck and a very good command of the Army language, besides being a Warwickshire man.

I am afraid however, that we of the Worcester's never forgave him for the Katia catastrophe and rightly or wrongly thought that if he had used the Warwick's more energetically he could have saved more of our chums who went under on Easter Sunday 1916.

The Hotchkiss gun inspection occupied us all morning and in the afternoon we joined the rest of the regiment in an inspection of all Arms followed by a saddlery inspection.

After a hasty tea, we saddled up and rode off to In Seirat again then spent the night on outpost in the trenches we had dug a few days previously. I think all who read this will agree that it was a most enjoyable Bank Holiday and we were not troubled with the usual worry of "how shall we spend the day?"

10ᵗʰ April 1917: My diary reminds me that on coming from the outpost, I fell sick with sun stroke and was ill for three days. This stroke was no doubt due to the hard work I had been putting in on the Hotchkiss and the very hot weather we had been experiencing.

We were bombed by Taubes several times. Stan Needham was wounded in the back by a fragment. The following week was spent on the usual tasks – an outpost near Sierat or Jemmi every other night. We had some good sea bathing, which was always a delight, as it was the only way we could keep clean – fresh water was scarce. This week we had startling news from our Troop Officer, Lieutenant Harvey (Martin) who announced that he and Lieutenant Parsons (the Warwickshire cricketer) were going to take a party each, gallop through the Turkish lines and cut the Beersheba to Gaza telegraph wires. It sounded rather absurd to us and we all thought it was asking for trouble. Although we had traversed the country and cut wires when we attacked Gaza on 26ᵗʰ March, it was a different proposition now for the Turks held this line in strength. The Turkish defence was not a continuous trench, but a series of trenched places in commanding positions. The idea of these 'raiders' was to find a way through the enemy outposts under cover of darkness, cut the wires, then gallop off.

I always regretted that I did not accompany the 'raiders', especially when they returned safe, sound and successful, but Lieutenant Harvey selected his party. When I asked why I was not included, he informed me that Major Straker wanted me for Hotchkiss gun work which I discovered was very true a few days later.

The raiding party from our troop consisted of 'Martin', Harold Wood, Alf Gilbert, Corporal John Mills, George Knight and Alf Davis. As I could not go, I lent my horse to Gilbert, whose old mare was rather slow.

The exploit was arranged for Monday 16th April and much amusement was aroused when Lieutenant Harvey turned up on parade with a useful looking 'bludgeon' instead of his sword.

32 - Left to right: Lieutenant Harvey; Sergeant T Nixon; G Knight; J Hanson; a Davis; J Mills; the last one unknown, the raiding party

The regiment paraded and marched off about 4.00 pm to Tel el Jemmi where we halted and off saddled for a couple of hours. Whilst resting, the raiding party stripped their saddles and themselves of everything except essentials in order that they could ride 'light'.

One of the parties gave me a few 'billet doux' with strict orders to destroy them if he did not return. Another (Alf Davis, I believe) gave me all his spare cash (about 4/-) saying that he would rather I had it than some dirty Turk.

About 11.00 pm we saddled up and moved across the Wadi Ghuzzi into Turkish territory. Our squadron separated from the regiment and accompanied the two raiding parties to their jumping-off place, which had previously been agreed on. Lieutenant Parson's party took a different direction to ours, the idea being that if one failed the other might succeed. We were there until daylight listening for rifle fire and wondering how our pals were faring.

As daylight broke, we rode forward in extended order towards the enemy and kept a sharp lookout for our small party, who soon appeared out of the morning mist galloping like hell. Their faces were dirty but happy. Martin carried some yards of telegraph wire to prove that they had done the job. Lieutenant Parsons' party galloped up shortly afterwards and were very disappointed when they heard that our lads had succeeded for they had ridden straight into a strong post of Turks. They retreated and then tried again but with the same result. They suffered a lame horse and Teddy Trigg had been thrown down a large hole and broken his collar bone.

The following account by E.V.G. was sent to the Marlborough Times on 8th June and published.

DARING RAID BY YEOMANRY.

We have been very busy, having taken part in a big attack on a very strong Turkish position. The grand assault was on 19th of April, but Johnny Turk refused to quit. They had a line across the main road between two old cities mentioned in the Bible.(Gaza/Beersheba.. omitted for security reasons)Along this road runs a telegraph wire and my troop officer was detailed off to go and cut it. As it was three miles behind the Turkish lines this was not an easy job. It was decided that the attempt should be made at night after the moon had sunk. The enemy trenches were not continuous but were dug in stretches of 20 to30 yards with intervals of about 200 yards in between. It would be Providence that guided our boys through one of these gaps. Our officer selected five of our best lads, mounted on picked horses, with instructions that every man should look after himself. Swords were only to be used on the outward journey, and coming home they should trust to luck and their horse's legs.

The squadron rode out at 1 a.m. We went out as far as we dare, until there was a danger of running into enemy outposts, as the raid was supposed to be a surprise. Our gallant boys rode off in the darkness, and we felt like cowards to see them go, never expecting to see them return. We thought of the little things they had asked us to do "in case anything happened".

As the night was pitchdark the direction had to be taken by compass readings, which necessitated several halts. The first mile was done at a steady trot, and all seemed serene when the leader held up his hands, and they pulled up short of the brink of a wadi or deep river bed with sides of about 40ft deep. This obstacle seemed to be insurmountable, until they luckily struck a path going down one side and up the other. While they were in the wadi, two Turks jumped up and ran for their lives. Had they fired it would have put the sentries behind them on the qui vive.

They now knew that they were in the enemy outpost line and would have to look out for trenches so they kept to the lowest parts of the valley. They quickened to a canter and passed several figures in the gloom, sticking close together, wondering if they would ever strike the wires. However, they kept their heads and at last struck rising ground. Up this slope at the gallop, and at the top they were rewarded by finding the road and just over it the wires.

Not a word by anyone; each man knew his work. One jumped up on to his saddle and standing up, reached a wire, out came the cutters and it was soon severed. To make certain, the wire was cut in several places, and a length removed, besides one or two insulators smashed. While this work was going on, eyes had to be kept open, and about 100 yards away one sentry was seen, absolutely frightened out of his life, for he crouched in the standing corn, not daring even to fire.

Everything being well done, the order to remount was given, and a race for liberty commenced. To hasten matters the dawn began to break, and if seen in the light the boys would certainly have been shot. Down the slope they came and were at once challenged by a Turk. Not stopping to argue with him, on they went. And now the Turks had got wind of someone being about, and rifle shots rang out from all directions. Several mounted men were passed, but they were apparently too timid to mount an attack and good progress was made, until one of the party fell into a deep hole, horse and all.

Two or three dismounted and hauled him up; into the saddle and away again. It was now getting light and the horses showing signs of fatigue when a long line of cavalry was spotted straight ahead. Their hearts sank, but they thought they might stand a chance so boldly galloped straight at the line. When nearing the others a cheer went up, for their own regiment was the so-thought enemy, and congratulations and handshakes met them in place of bullets.

I venture to say that the above true tale will never find a place in the big papers, like the trench raids in Flanders, but for six men to go out as they did, with their lives in their hands, and to get back successful and scatheless, was a brilliant piece of work. I am sorry to say that I was not in the wire-cutting business even though I asked the troop officer if I could be chosen.

17th April 1917: Still in reserve, we changed position several times and had a big gallop to and from a watering place which was under shell fire.

19th April 1917: 2nd Gaza battle: We left our bivouacs at 2.00 am and marched until daybreak. We dismounted and left our horses with the horse-holders. Our brigade was set the task of attacking the Atawini Redoubt, a low hill which commanded a large stretch of flat country over which we had to advance.

Atawini was well trenched and held by about 2,000 Turks and a Battery that we discovered afterwards. Our brigade strength (dismounted) would be about 700-800, so we had a tough job ahead.

The whole of the Turkish line was being attacked simultaneously. The Infantry and tanks at Gaza and Sheik Abbas, the Cavalry (dismounted) on the rest of the line, almost to Beersheba – a front of nearly 20 miles.

The Turks had made all preparations to receive us for we had given them three week notice and they had, of course, selected the best possible positions during that time and made ready miles of good deep trenches. We left the horses well out of artillery range and had quite a walk before we saw 'Jacko'. This would have been okay if we had enjoyed a nice rasher and a couple of eggs before we started! But as it was, we had been on the move all night and our breakfast consisted of 'bully' and biscuits swilled down with cold water (sparingly); with this done, we advanced.

I had a heavy load to labour under for I carried the Hotchkiss everywhere we went – we gunners were in great demand. The Turks allowed us to come well in range, then they let us have it – shrapnel and HE fast and furious. The 5.9 shells dropped several of our boys early on. I saw Joe Matthews in the next troop to ours, killed. Bert Ricketts and Tom Nixon wounded. We pushed on and were soon within rifle range (about 1,000 yards). Lying on our faces for a breather, with bullets dropping all round us, we began to wonder if we should ever live to get up to the Turkish trenches where we could plainly see the Turks firing at us.

Luckily someone discovered a deep watercourse about 100 yards ahead and we were soon in it. This turned out to be quite a roomy place, comfortably accommodating the whole of our brigade as, in some places; the sides were 15-20 feet deep. We sorted ourselves out, counted casualties then climbed out of our refuge and commenced to advance up the rising ground towards the enemy.

The Turks let us have it hot and strong, men fell on all sides, the rifle fire was terrific, I could never understand how any of us survived. We got down in the grass and returned the fire with the Hotchkiss and rifle, but it made little impression. During this phase of the fight, Major French-Blake was shot through the head and died immediately. *(See photo and extracts in Appendix)* (His diary is in the W Y Trust collection)

Doug Kerr of "D" Squadron was killed and Lieutenant Hagi, Lieutenant Featherstone and many more were wounded.

Our advance was checked so we retired to our little ravine again, where we got busy filling strips for the Hotchkiss guns.

It was just as well, for we had barely finished when we were ordered out on top again and found to our amazement that Jacko was not waiting on the hill for us, but was coming down to meet us in hundreds!

Apparently he was doing the same on our left, for we were surprised to see the Australian brigade next to us mount their horses and gallop away. Our right flank was covered by the HAC battery behind us who were firing with beautiful precision. Our interest was now centred on these cheeky fellows advancing towards us. Five of us with Hotchkiss guns found a good place to plant ourselves and with the aid of our teams, we were soon pouring a very hot fire into the advancing Turks. With five machine guns you can put up a very useful barrage and I am pleased to say that we stopped them at 200 yards and they broke and fled. I remember many small things that happened to me, for I was thoroughly strung up, but cool enough to know that aim and accuracy were most important at this time.

I recollect a fat Turkish Officer whom I dropped at about 400 yards. I can now see the light canvas uniforms with bright brass buttons and the Turks firing at us from their hips as they advanced. We continued to fire at them whenever we could see one or two, but they did not come again. The 6th Yeomanry Brigade came up on our left, so we felt very much relieved but had not captured Atawini. We stayed on till dusk when firing gradually died down. After collecting our dead and wounded, we retired about a half mile and waited for the horses – very glad that THAT day was over.

EXTRACT FROM THE REGIMENTAL HISTORY,p 101.

THE SECOND BATTLE OF GAZA was over.The casualty list was nearly 12,000, falling as usual on the Infantry, which included the Worcestershire Regiment. The Camel Corps and 3rd& 4th Australian Horse Brigades suffered considerably also, but the remainder of the Cavalry got off comparatively lightly.

The Worcs.Yeomanry lost a fine Squadron leader, a Regular Army soldier from the 21st Lancers, Maj. StJ. Ffrench-Blake.He had already been in action on the Western front in 1914.

Corporal Kerr and Troopers Matthews and Crutchley were killed and 19 badly wounded. The Regiment was saved from defeat by the brave action of three Berkshire Yeomanry squadrons and one of the Bucks, who lost their Colonel in the repulse to relieve the broken left flank. We retired to El Mendur, a small Arab village about 4 miles back where the whole of our Division seemed to be. We were all absolutely done up after the gruelling day's fighting, preceded by three sleepless nights. On the march, most of us fell asleep in the saddle. McDonald, our Signaller, not only fell asleep but he also fell down a large hole about 12 feet deep, horse and all, but it did not seem to hurt him. As he could not get his horse out of it, he decided to spend the rest of the night in the best possible way that was by sleeping beside his horse. Before lying down, however, he stuck up one of his signalling flags so that no one else would fall on top of him. Sometime later he was awakened by shouting and on answering 'Hello', he was asked "Is this Divisional Headquarters?"

The question was asked in good faith, for it was a dark night and no doubt the questioner thought he had struck the entrance to a huge cave where the General had taken up his abode. We sent out a rescue party as soon as it was light and dug Mac and his horse out, none the worse for his fall. After a brew of tea and a snack of 'bully', we saddled up again and moved to Munkeileh, two miles from Atawini position. The horses were left in charge of a few men and the rest of us set to work digging trenches on a bit of high ground. After a hard day's work we were rewarded by a night on outpost in a very high wind, near the White Tomb of Munkeileh. The following day was spent digging near the tomb and that night we were actually allowed to sleep in a reserve trench. This was the first night's sleep we had for five nights. Considering the hard work we had put in during the week, it will be understood how done up we all were.

Chapter 19

22nd April 1917: We trekked out to the White Tomb* to put the finishing touches to our trenches. We also buried the horses that had been killed in the battle four days ago. At dusk we moved off to Abassan el Kebir, 10 miles in the direction of the coast.

The following day, however, it was discovered that there was insufficient water for us, so we moved to Beni Sela near Khan Yunis where there was plenty of water. We remained here for two days, on one of which the whole regiment marched down to the sea coast and enjoyed a bathe, which we all needed.

☐ *See Lord Hampton paintings*

26th April 1917: A hot Khamseen wind blew all day. We moved to El Shauth, the prepared Turkish position about which we had heard rumours when we were at El Arish some months back.

We were all astonished at the strength of the defences and were pleased that we had not been called on to attack this position. A feature of the defence was a line of deep bowls, evidently dug to stop a cavalry charge. From inscriptions on the walls of the dug-outs we gathered that this place was the work of Armenian and Jewish civilian prisoners, which turned out to be correct.

Whilst at El Shauth, we set to work to adopt the Turkish position to our requirements, which meant that we had to turn the back to the front etc. In addition to the everlasting digging, our horses had to be attended to and as water was three miles away in the Wadi Ghuzzi, this meant travelling 12 miles per day.

On the second day the temperature, which had been well over 100 degrees, suddenly fell to 60 degrees due to a sea breeze, for which were very grateful, for many of us (myself included) were suffering from a touch of sunstroke.

30th April 1917: The routine at El Shauth was: Reveille 3.30 am, saddle up and get ready to mount (with a day's ration for man and horse packed), 'stand to' until 5.00 am, off saddle and dig until 8.30 am, breakfast, take horses to water (this takes about 2½ hrs), groom horses, feed, dinner, digging from 2.00 – 5.30 pm, feed horses, tea, rest of time to yourself. Rations were very short; if you wanted to wash you had to find a new nosebag. If you had two pints left after 3 miles from the Wadi, where you had filled the nosebag, you were lucky.

The regiment soon began to feel the effects of this regime, for men started falling sick every day as they were absolutely worn out. This made things harder for those of us who remained well.

Major Straker left us looking very ill, my pal Jack Mills also went to hospital. We did not see Jack again until December, for whilst down at Cairo, he got leave and had a trip home.

3rd May 1917: We moved from El Shauth back to Beni Sela. We were given a treat the next day. We were taken down to the Railhead at Khan Yunis and thoroughly disinfected or 'de-loused' as the wags called it. The process was as follows: two railway wagons and an engine were the baths, we undressed by the wagons, tied up our clothes in a bundle, the bundles were then packed into the wagon nearest the engine, doors closed, then steam was forced through everything at high pressure.

While this was going on, as many men as possible got into the other wagon and had a good bath. It was an extremely funny sight to see dozens of men in their birthday suits, except that we all kept our big sun helmets on. After half hour steaming, the kits were thrown out of the steamer, we opened them to the sun for two or three minutes, dressed, saddled up and rode back to camp feeling very much cleaner and comfortable.

This disinfecting was a jolly good idea and we all welcomed it. But it was not done frequently enough. I believe I went through it four times in 3½ years on the desert, probably the Infantry used it more often, because we mounted troops were not often near the railway.

5th May 1917: My 30th birthday which we celebrated the occasion in Eric Shorthouse's bivouac in the Machine Gun Corps. 'Shorty' left us for England on this day, where he was given a Commission and sent to France. We did not see him again till '*Apres la Guerre*'.

8th May 1917 : We moved down to Marakeb, a flat stretch of sand on the sea shore where, needless to say, we indulged in the luxury of a swim two or three times a day. The bathing was good but dangerous owing to the strong currents. One or two men drowned while we were there. Bill Harvey from Birmingham got into difficulties one morning and was half drowned before two or three of us swam out and got him ashore.

I did my best with the Hotchkiss gun whilst here, but did not have much support from the Squadron Leader, Captain Brown, a little chap who had been in charge of '**D**' Squadron after Major Straker left. Captain Brown remained with us until August.

Luckily for us it was not a very dangerous time while he was in charge, for he could not have managed a Sunday school treat. He faded away down the line shortly before the fighting began and we did not see his dapper little form again. We had a touch of civilisation introduced whilst at Marakeb, for we actually had a cinema show one evening. I believe we had the Brigade Chaplain to thank for this.

15th May 1917: We packed up and moved west across a high line of sand hills that separated the sea shore from the flat country inland. Halfway across the sand hills, I was suddenly taken ill with acute pains in my "little Mary" which made it difficult to sit on my horse. I 'fell out' and a pal stayed with me.

It was a sudden attack of colic, but I was able to ride after an hour or two's rest. We found the regiment at Abbasan el Kebir. Just as we were having our tea, a terrible dust storm blew up and covered everything with a film of light brown powder. This was our first taste of these storms. We'd had sand storms on the desert, but these dust storms almost choked you and it was impossible to keep the food clean. We had many more before the summer of 1917 was over, particularly when we camped near Tel el Fara.

These dust storms did not improve my colic and I experienced other attacks with the result that on 17th May, Dr. Teichmann sent me back to Marakeb to a rest camp for tired soldiers of the Desert Mounted Corps.

17th May 1917: I made my journey (about 6 miles) by camel and quite enjoyed the trip. I had a fortnight in the camp, which did me a heap of good. It was a real rest camp; these affairs are usually misnomers in the Army and are generally drill camps.

We had absolutely nothing to do except to see the Doctor at 10.00 am every morning. The Red Cross Society had fixed up a library, the sea was at our door and the food was clean and good.

I met Dr. Torrance here, a good man who looked after our brigade on Gallipoli after Dr. Teichmann was wounded. He was a humane person and did not suspect everyone of malingering, or if he did, he was sensible enough to disguise it.

It was Dr. Torrance who ordered me down to the Field Hospital on Gallipoli in September 1915.

Dr. Teichmann knew every man in the regiment personally and could guess a man's complaint without asking him any questions. It was a good thing we had such men up the line with us, for I met some queer Medicals in some of the hospitals.

Major Teichman D.S.O.,M.C., Croix de Guerre, was Medical Officer from 1914-1918. He was wounded by shrapnel at Suvla Bay, in August 1915 and again at Romani, Sinai, in August 1916, he was wounded while was attending to casualties.

He was then promoted in 1918 to Lieutenant Colonel in charge of a Military Hospital in Italy.(His war diary is in the WYMuseum Collection).

I remained at the rest camp until 25th May, then returned to the regiment just in time for a minute inspection of the Hotchkiss guns by the Colonel at which I had to answer questions as nothing had been done in my absence. At this time each Troop Officer was responsible for his own gun. If an Officer was not particularly interested in the gun then it suffered from neglect, unless a keen man like Buckman of No. 1 Troop or H. Roberts of No. 4 Troop looked after it.

28th May 1917 : (Whit Monday) – we packed up and moved further inland to Tel el Fara, about 7 or 8 miles away. After getting some rest for a few hours, we were roused at 11.00 pm and marched off with the rest of the Brigade at 1.00 am towards the Turks. We carried out a 'recce' towards the Turkish positions north of Karno and approached as near as we could without getting into a scrap. However, Johnny Turk was roused and came after us, but as were not fighting that day, we withdrew. Our Squadron was the 'lucky one' left behind to cover the brigade, so it fell to us to stop the Turks coming on too fast. This is never a nice job and we were all relieved when we received orders to mount and ride for 'home' - we arrived at tea time, tired and thirsty.

1st June 1917: We took part in another reconnaissance, this time towards Beersheba. We did not come into contact with the enemy on this journey, for we went about 10 miles up the Wadi Ghuzzi to a spot called Rachid Bek. Apparently the Turks left the country around here to look after itself. Indeed they were not bad judges for it was nothing but rocks and big stones, with deep ravines running in all directions – absolutely impassable. When we attacked Beersheba three months later, we made a wide detour to avoid this district although it lay in the direct route to our objective.

After spending the night and the following morning floundering about in this no-mans land, we withdrew about midday and off-saddled for an hour at Bir el Esani, where we found water for the men and horses.

During this halt, I recollect an absurd row which took place between Neal and Stokes, culminating in a fight. The temperature was well over 100 degrees and we had all been on the go for well over 24 hours, tempers were short under these conditions. We soon separated the combatants.

These rides into fresh country, although trying, were really oases in the desert of days of the same routine for weeks on end. They comprised outposts at Karno, watering horses twice a day in the Wadi, Hotchkiss gun lessons for me and my class – all in a day's work. The Brigade Chaplain was a Trier, for he managed to get a piano up the line, so we had one or two camp concerts. The weather was terribly hot and we only had our little bivouac sheets to crawl under for shade.

Those horrible dust storms were constantly blowing, generally at meal times, with the result that the health of the troops worsened as each day passed. These arduous conditions were recognised at Headquarters, for the rest camp at Marakeb was now an established institution. Any man not quite up to the mark was sent down if the Medical Officer said so. I worked very hard at Fara with the Hotchkiss classes in addition to the usual outposts, stables etc. I finally 'broke down' after a trying day and two nights on outpost. I packed up and went to the Field (Brigade) Hospital with Jack Garside - probably a touch of sunstroke.

24th June 1917: We were both sent down to the rest camp (in sand carts, not camels) and remained in the camp until 6th July when our regiment came down to Marakeb for a rest. We rejoined them the same day. Our days up at Tel el Fara, as I said before, were monotonous, for although in touch with the Turks, no one seemed to know exactly what we were doing. We were certainly watching Johnny and knew he was watching us, but neither side appeared to have a plan of attack.

Were we going to take Gaza for the third time or had we reached our limit in Palestine? Our Officers knew nothing. It may have been that Captain Brown had his own ideas about letting those under him know what the main plan was.

If he had, it was very short-sighted of him. The best Officers, Major Wiggin and Lord Hampton always made a point of explaining everything about the campaign to us, with the idea that every man could take an intelligent interest in what he was called on to do.

WC3 - Watercolour by Lord Hampton: Brigade HQ at Tel el Fara

As I have remarked, the campaign seemed to have reached deadlock when one day we had a 'bombshell' dropped, General Allenby was coming out to take command; now things were going to liven up! Up to this time, Sir Archibald Murray (and Lady Murray) conducted the operations from Cairo some 200 miles away in the Savoy Hotel. No doubt the orders issued were known to an intelligent enemy as soon as they were to the men at the front. Egypt was a hotbed of spies, pro Turks were everywhere.

The manager of Shepheard's Hotel, much frequented by our Officers, was an Austrian and he probably extracted a great deal of information before he was interned.

I am pleased to say that the first thing that General Allenby did on his arrival, was to move GHQ up to Khan Yunis about 15 miles from the front line. We felt then that our GOC was with us.

Chapter 20

General Allenby takes command

7th July 1917: General Allenby visited all the outposts that we held. After a small review of the troops in our vicinity, he went right along the line to Gaza.

He was a man who inspired confidence. The very fact of the GOC having a look at the front line was unheard of up till then. It was not too much to say that his personality had a great deal to do with the success he achieved in Palestine.

Sir Archibald Murray was a figurehead to us, no more in the front line than Kitchener, but Allenby was a real live GOC moving about amongst us. He frequently stopped his motor car to pick up Tommie's who were slogging on foot.

He earned our gratitude by ordering all the beer in Egypt up to the men in the front line when he discovered we could not get it. Only small matters when viewed from an armchair in England, but big things to us in those dry, dusty days in Palestine.

Until the arrival of General Allenby, Sir Philip Chetwode was GOC on the desert. We certainly saw a good deal of him, for he was constantly amongst us. During the battle of Rafa in January 1917, I saw him under fire, looking very keen.

We remained at Marakeb by the sea until 14th August. The weather was extremely hot, but we were compensated by the good bathing which we enjoyed daily. We were not idle during this time for the horses had plenty of attention and Hotchkiss training was the order of the day. Colonel Williams and Major Wiggin organised a very good Hotchkiss competition consisting of, galloping into action, firing at targets, changing positions, attending to mechanical faults, changing hot barrels and finally galloping back to the starting point.

Marks were given for hits on the targets, time occupied, correct orders to loader, horse holder and general procedure. Every troop in the regiment took part. My team consisted of: No. 1 self; No. 2 Alf Davis; No. 3 Fearn and Bert Morris (the horse holder).

We did very well in the first and second rounds, easily beating our opponents, but in the final run off we came to grief and just managed to get into third place. We were first favourites in the betting and we were rather disgusted with ourselves! Nobody in particular was to blame, except perhaps my shooting was not as good as it should have been.

The horses were not as quiet as usual and we accidentally knocked sand into the gun which jammed it. The competition was won by H. Roberts Team (D Squadron) with 38 points (50 hits on target); second place by J. Littlehales with 31 points (40 hits); and third, my team with 29 points (31 hits).

This competition took place on the sand hills on the 11th August 1917 and after dashing about on loose sand carrying a machine gun with the thermometer somewhere over 100 degrees, the reader will readily believe that we must have been very keen.

27th July 1917: General Chauvel, the Australian Commander of the Desert Mounted Corps, to which we belonged, paid the camp a visit to look at men and horses.

28th July 1917: The Director of Medical Services had us lined up for inspection. The inspection was very humorous for we heard that General Allenby was astonished at the state of health in which he found the troops. It was really an eye-opener for anyone new to the desert. Every man in the fighting forces was covered in septic sores on their hands, faces and legs - all in bandages. My own hands did not properly heal until the cold weather in December. All this trouble was no doubt due to the poor state of our blood.

If one's hand was accidentally knocked against a saddle, a large piece of skin came off. The result was an open sore that would not heal. The swarms of flies settling on the sore did not improve matters, so we had to use bandages for self-preservation. To continue about the inspection by the DMS, we were formed into three ranks. The first line were 'bad' cases, wrecks etc. The second line 'fairly bad' and the rear rank 'not so bad'. The old

MO seemed surprised at some of the men that he saw, but no doubt other regiments had shown him the same sorry state of affairs.

He enquired as to what we thought would help in this matter and the almost unanimous reply was that we wanted a supply of canteen goods and some beer.

The inspection evidently bore fruit, for canteen goods soon arrived up the line and we were able to buy eggs, tinned fruit, chocolate etc. And for anyone who wanted it, a pint of beer in the evening.

This seemed to be the inauguration of the canteen movement on the desert. Prior to this date, Eric Cowley was despatched to Port Said occasionally to buy a stock of goods which he had great difficulty in bringing back up to the front line. Henceforth the Navy and Army Canteen Board opened stores at convenient places and you could always count on obtaining good food at reasonable prices.

9th August 1917: Brigade Horse Show - Sergeant 'Farmer' Allen did very well.

13th August 1917: A Field Day was held at In Seirat on some high ground towards Gaza. We had one of the old fashioned schemes that we used to enjoy in England, knocking one another out of action with flags etc.

14th August 1917: We packed our saddles and trekked off down the line to El Arish halting one night at Rafa and one night at El Burj. At El Arish we pitched our 'bivvies' in a fig orchard. The figs were just ripening so we had dessert all day long!

WP2 - Watercolour by Lord Hampton of Brigade HQ at Marakeb

Chapter 21

Lord Hampton took over "D" Squadron: He remained our O/C until we were demobilised. We had not seen a lot of him on active service for he had been on the Brigade Staff.

At the time we all felt rather doubtful as to what kind of a leader he would make; a Squadron Leader can do a lot of good or harm to his men. Lord Hampton proved to be a real gentleman. He was a brave leader in action and a considerate man when we were down the line in rest camps.

17th August 1917: We were all inoculated against Typhoid Fever and, as before, I was bowled over for a day or two.

This was not surprising as E V Godrich was more than immune from typhoid by virtue of his life threatening infection in Gallipoli.

19th August 1917: We moved camp about half a mile from the fig orchard to a shady little place under a clump of date palms near the seashore. The dates were plentiful but not ripe enough to eat with safety. Soon after we moved to this camp, about half the regiment was sent down the line to Port Said where a rest camp had been opened for mounted troops. On their return, the remainder of us were sent down for a holiday.

30th August 1917: We found a very comfortable camp on the seashore run by Australian Officers (not much discipline). Port Said is not a very large place, but it was a nice change for us to have a touch of civilisation.

We found one or two decent restaurants and lived like human beings for a few days. The Continental Hotel, Hotel de la Poste and YMCA were all patronised. One afternoon, two or three of us hired a small boat and sailed down the Suez Canal to a camp of Armenian refugees. These people were the remnants of a massacre in Asia Minor and had been rescued by American ships. They were engaged in weaving, woodworking, lace making and other industries by which they earned sufficient to keep themselves.

The day following our sail, I had a game of tennis in the morning and in the afternoon I got between my blankets with a temperature. I went to see the MO the following morning and was at once packed off to the 31st General Hospital with tonsillitis.

I felt disgusted with myself at spoiling a good holiday in this fashion, but found on arrival at hospital that there was quite an epidemic of throat trouble in the town.

6th September 1917 (General Hospital): I was here from 6th to 17th September. It was nicely situated on the eastern side of the Canal, i.e. opposite side to Port Said. It was a block of buildings normally used as the offices of the Suez Canal Company and as the rooms were lofty and cool, the place lent itself admirably for a Hospital. The canal docks ran right into the heart of the hospital, so we did not have far to go for a swim. Whilst I was there a swimming gala was organised and provided a good afternoon's entertainment. I was lucky enough to find a real good Dentist at the hospital who attended to my teeth as they were in need of treatment.

Some years later I discovered that my Australian cousin, whom I had never met, died in this hospital on 11th April 1918. He was Harry Godrich of the 10th Australian Light Horse Regiment.

17th – 27th September 1917: I was at Kantara Base waiting until a sufficient number of our regiment arrived to make up a party.

Most of my time was spent with Tommy Bickerton and Alf Gilbert, who had also been in hospital. Our chief amusement was bathing and walking over the bridge to a soldier's restaurant for a good supper every night. I also played cards with J. Bunegar, who was killed at Huj six weeks later.

We left Kantara on a troop train (open trucks packed in like herrings) at about 4.30 pm and arrived at El Arish at 3.30 am (about 100 miles). Not being fond of night walks, we dumped our kits on the platform (sand) and slept until about 7.00 am.

We then trekked off to where we had left the regiment a month previous. We were astonished to find that the 'birds had flown' - luckily our Brigade Headquarters remained.

We discovered Phil Everett, Harold Williams and others who made us welcome and gave us a good breakfast. We then caught a train during the morning which took us to Wadi Sheik Noran on the branch line towards Beersheba where we telephoned the regiment for horses, which soon arrived.

28th September 1917: We joined the regiment at Tel el Fara where the Division had taken over the outpost line under canvas. After a day's rest, we went on outpost duty. The following night we rested.

2nd October 1917: We went out as a covering party to the Senior Officers of the 74th Division (dismounted Yeomanry) who were taking a look at the positions that they were to attack in the forthcoming operations.

We rode well within rifle shot and could plainly see the Turks in the trenches. We also frightened several cavalry outposts who did not stay to argue. These positions were the main Turkish defences covering Beersheba, the trenches were on high ground in very rough country and commanded a very good field of fire over which our Infantry would advance. We felt sorry for the 74th Division and could foresee a heavy casualty list.

This, however, did not prove to be the case, for when the attack was made, Johnny Turk had two divisions of Australians and Yeomanry round at his back door and did not defend his beautifully prepared positions with much heart!

We hung about inviting the enemy to put a machine gun on us whilst the Infantry Officers marked their maps, took distances and compass bearings etc. To make matters worse, two curious gentlemen went so far forward that they got lost, were nearly captured and delayed our return until darkness had fallen.

The result was that we had to go very gingerly for several miles over rough country. We arrived back at camp at about 1.00 am, a journey of some 35 miles, which made me feel stiff for a day or two.

8th October 1917: Today we commenced a Musketry Course at El Ghabi, a few miles south. A good range had been constructed and we had several good days shooting, both with the Hotchkiss and the rifle. Jack Knight from Pershore topped the Squadron scores. I was placed 6th in the Squadron with the rifle.

18th October 1917: We made another strong reconnaissance, this time to Wadi Imleh. This country was very interesting because it was the ground from which the Turkish Cavalry outposts watched us every day, but that evening we had the pleasure of using their watering places at Bir Iflis. We had a good look round their position and noticed a fine viaduct that carried their new railway line from Gaza to Beersheba.

19th October 1917: I was confirmed at Shellal by the Bishop of Jerusalem. The ceremony took place in a marquee erected for the occasion. There were about 200 men received.

The Service was impressive, for we all knew that fighting was to commence shortly and realised that this might be the last Service that some of us would take part in. I took my first Communion on the following Sunday in the little tent of our Brigade Chaplain.

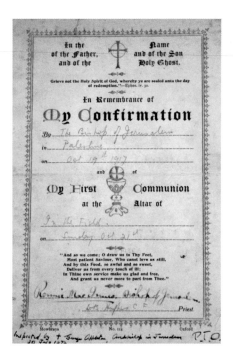

The following week passed by quietly. Saddlery and kit were overhauled, poor horses sent away with poor men to a convenient 'dump'. We struck camp, packed up, drew as much food and fodder as would could pack in our saddles for as Quartermaster Bill Walker said, "God knows when or where you will get the next lot from".

27th October 1917: We saddled up and marched off up the Wadi to Esani (about 10 miles) and took up an outpost line near Rashid Bek, just before dawn.

When the mist cleared we could see the Turkish outposts across the valley, but neither side opened fire. We were withdrawn the following night and marched on in darkness to Maalagu, where we pegged down the horses and had a night's sleep.

Chapter 22

Battle of Beersheba

29th October 1917: We saddled up early and marched on Khalasa (6 miles) where we pulled out again after watering our horses. At dawn we were sent out several miles on patrol towards the enemy but found everything to be quiet.

30th October 1917: I was sent on about 2.00 pm with an Officer of Corps Headquarters to Asluy, the next halting place. This was in order that I could act as a guide to our brigade when they arrived in the middle of the night. It turned out to be a beautifully clear night with a full moon, so my services were not much in demand. The horses were given a mouthful of water, and we marched on towards Beersheba. We discovered that the Anzac Division, and the rest of our Division, had already moved off. As we knew that the attack commenced at dawn, the inference was that our brigade had clicked for reserves.

31st October 1917: Our surmise proved to be correct, for as soon as dawn broke, heavy firing started a mile or two from us, so we knew that the Anzac Division was attacking. On the left across the hills we could hear the Artillery of the 74th Division pounding away at the trenches that we had studied a few weeks back.
We halted and dismounted on a big hill which commanded a good view of the country northwards. The country was very hilly and very grand. Great deep valleys ran in all directions, hill after hill rising up to one great fellow whose summit was lost in the clouds.
I well remember Harold Wood and myself getting out our maps and compasses trying to place this high mountain, when Billie Lane (who had been promoted from Sergeant to 2nd Lieutenant a week before) came along and told us that the hill was Ras el Narg, 2000 feet high. Billie was killed on this very hill three days later.

We remained in this position, shivering with the cold in the early mists, snatched a bit of bully and biscuits and at about 10.00 am mounted and moved on a further 2-3 miles towards the firing.
We dismounted again in a valley with hills on either side and remained here until dusk. It was a most depressing day because

we could see nothing of the battle. We could hear the incessant firing just over the hill in front. We kept wondering when on earth they would call for the reserves to finish off the day. The call never came, but several German airmen did and they gave us a very warm time, killing a number of horses. I do not know how many men were hit.

When darkness had fallen, we mounted and marched off to a Wadi to water the horses. We found a few little puddles, but the poor beasts could not get much out of them and after hanging about for a few more hours, we pushed on and marched over the battle ground into Beersheba – we arrived just before dawn on 1st November.

We were bombed again while we were halted near the Wadi Saba, but little damage was done. After the Colonel had spied out the land, he found some neat little stalls and dug-outs that had been vacated the previous day by the Turkish cavalry.

We soon appropriated these and found them very comfortable. They had even cut mangers for the horses feed, but better still they had left us huge stores of corn and tibbin (chopped straw). We were not long collecting all this in our blankets and our horses had as much to eat as they could for the next few days.

The engineers got to work on the wells and soon had the pumps working with the result that we had an ample water supply. We found plenty of wood, so were able to boil our 'Dixies' and have tea four or five times a day.

All this was very nice after our hardship of the previous five days. We were all hoping that we would be in this Beersheba Garrison for a long time, but the GOC thought otherwise, for after 2 days rest we moved off.

3rd November 1917: At 9.00 am we marched north to Ras el Narg, about 20 miles. We took up a very exposed position on some rough hills. We had to gallop the last part under heavy rifle and machine gun fire from Khuwelfeh where the 53rd Division was trying to dislodge a strong enemy position. The hills were so steep that we dismounted and helped our horses over the boulders and large rocks.

We finally found a valley which protected the horses from the heavy fire. Here we left them and clambered up to the top of the hill and relieved the 2nd Australian Brigade, who appeared absolutely exhausted. They were very pleased to see us. After they had gone we found we were 'up against it' as there were plenty of Turks in front and their shooting was good.

We got all the shelter that we could find behind the large rocks, but they soon started potting us off. Bill Lane was killed, Fred Darby was hit in four places, Harry Skudder stopped a nasty one in the throat, Lieutenant 'Martin' Harvey got one through his heel, but pluckily carried on until his foot became numb. We got our Hotchkiss and machine guns going and gave them back as much as we received. The firing went on thick and heavy until dusk.

As darkness fell, so the noise died down and we were able to sit up and think about the inner man. We soon realised that we were in a nasty place, apart from the bullets, for the only available water was at Beersheba (20 miles away). It was a case of self-denial with a vengeance.

A fearful thirst in your mouth, a pint of water in your bottle which was dangling on your chest and you have to keep saying to yourself, NO, NO, but towards midnight we were told that a water cart had arrived so we went down with a load of bottles.

We were given another pint which lasted us for the next 24 hours (all through the following day under a merciless sun which made the rocks so hot that you could not touch them).

When we were not shooting Turks, we had time to look around at the scenery. The most interesting view was to the north which included the Beersheba to Jerusalem Road.

Several miles up this road, on a hill, was a large Arab town, its white walls shining bright in the sun. We discovered later that this was the Ancient City of Hebron, mentioned in the Bible several times.

4th November 1917: At dawn we were relieved by the Warwick's, so we went down below to the horses. We spent a wretched day in Reserve listening to the Warwick's up on the hill top, blazing away.

About 3.00 pm we hurriedly mounted, rode down our valley and up another one, where we climbed on foot up the hills just in time to help the Gloucester's repel a very determined attack. The Turks appeared to be all cavalry, riding up to within ½ mile of us, dismounted and then came on foot.

We let them have it hot and strong, they soon had enough when they reached a few hundred yards distance and we could knock them over pretty well, although I thought we were in for a bit of bayonet work. We had several false alarms, but this was the last kick. They then galloped away on their little ponies with their long tails flying in the breeze.

We were relieved just before dusk by the New Zealand Mounted Rifles. We were more than glad to see them for we had been through two gruelling days. We suffered 30 casualties and were all half dead with thirst.

I remember Lord Hampton was very ill during the second day; he was suffering from thirst but would not touch the bottles that several of us offered him. Thirst knocked over Ernie Rogers, George Hinton and several others. Some of us had a drop of water but did not know when the next lot would arrive, so kept it safe. After the New Zealanders took over, we set off on our march back to Beersheba (and water) about 20 miles away. We arrived at 4.00 am on the morning of 5th November.

On arrival at Beersheba, we went straight to the water troughs which were filled with the precious liquid. The horses drank and drank until I thought they would burst.

We got down on our knees and drank our fill as well, in spite of warnings of Cholera etc. I shall never forget our two thirsty days at Ras el Narg and whenever I see beautiful English water running to waste; my mind goes back to those terrible hours of agony when men would have sold their souls for water, only water.

The remainder of the day was spent resting, for both horses and men were done up. We took our places in the Turkish dug-outs again and had a good night's sleep.

6th November 1917: We woke up refreshed and comparatively new men. After breakfast we set off in all directions to see what the Turks had left in Beersheba.

We found souvenirs of all sorts that would have looked very well on the sideboard at home but unfortunately they do not provide wagons for souvenirs for men who do the dirty work in the front line. That privilege is reserved for the people who came along a few days later, when all is safe.

I can truthfully say however, that the majority of the boys of our regiment were chiefly concerned with finding corn and tibben for their horses. Two or three of our Squadron came across a small herd of goats and caught one. It was brought home and slaughtered and we all had a piece of meat. We cooked it in many different ways but it was too hard to eat – a terrible disappointment.

At teatime we were informed that we were moving on that night, so we packed our saddles with as much food for horse and man as they would hold, once again being told "God knows when you will get the next supply". At 1.00 am we saddled up and marched off through Beersheba and steered a westerly course behind the trenches that the Turks had so carefully prepared. We had learnt that the whole line from Beersheba to Gaza (30 miles) was being gradually rolled up, so we knew we were going to indulge in a game of "hunt the Turk" in open country.

The stand at Kuwelfeh and Ras el Narg was a clever blind by the enemy to draw a large body of troops against them to the detriment of the main attack on the Gaza position. General Allenby refused to be drawn that way and only sent the 53rd (Welsh) Division, the Camel Corps and our Division.

We all had a very rough time and lost of lot of good men, but while we were holding out against a superior enemy, our main Army was pushing on which forced the Turks at Ras el Narg to retreat towards Jerusalem.

7th November 1917: When dawn broke we found ourselves with the Infantry, who were advancing extended in skirmishing order. We discovered that they were the 60th (London) Division. We advanced on their left flank until about 3.00 pm when we arrived near Sheria Wells.

This was the only water for miles, but Johnny Turk was shelling the place like fury – having only just been thrown out, he knew all about it. As soon as it was dark we managed to get near the wells and almost fought our way to the water – there were thousands of men and horses all desperate for it.

By the time we had watered all the horses and had a bit of bully beef, the night was half gone and a nap on the ground holding your horse's rein is not refreshing.

8th November: This will always be remembered as a Red Letter Day in our regimental history. At dawn, we tightened our girths and marched off, still acting as left flank guard to the 60th Division. We had not been in touch with the enemy the previous day except for his shelling, but we all anticipated some dirty work today – we were not disappointed.

We had not proceeded far when our Squadron was separated from "A" and "C" squadrons, who went with the Colonel to the right flank of the Infantry to join a Squadron of the Warwick's.

I remember a little incident here. We were halted but "A" and "C" squadrons had just continued moving when suddenly Captain (Toby) Albright of 'A' shouted jokingly across to us *"don't forget to watch the point of the sword"* (a Barrack instruction). Poor Toby was killed a few hours later; he was a good Officer, a gentleman and a very loveable man who had a joke or a cheery word for the humblest private.

After the other two squadrons had left, we carried on with our flank guard work. Our Leader, Lord Hampton, sent first one troop and then another, two or three miles away to a village or a hill to have a look round to see if any Turks were about.

We captured several bunches of the enemy like this as they were tired, hungry and had lost their regiments. The best capture we made was of two small mules with goatskins full of water. This was good as we had not seen any water since leaving Sheria Wells, the night before.

The two mules went with us everywhere after this. Lord Hampton used them to carry his kit, thus releasing a horse. He named them Abdul and Joey. Although they were bags of bones when we found them, Stan Naylor soon had them sleek and fat (Stan was Lord Hampton's groom).

We rode steadily on, mile after mile, over gently undulating country, something like Salisbury Plain, until about 3.00 pm when we came to a rise in the ground. We halted before climbing the hill to expose ourselves. Lord Hampton called for a Corporal and one man (I was sent with Harry Cooks).

The three of us walked on foot to the top of the hill, we saw in front of us a valley 4-5 miles across. In the dip was a large camp of tents and a bit of brickwork.

Around the camp, two or three dozen square heaps, that we made out to be ammunition dumps. Through the glasses we could see a few Turks hurrying about and scores of them climbing the hill on the far side of the valley, evidently having left the camp a short time before.

Lord Hampton then sent Corporal Sandover and three men to reconnoitre. He told them to be careful and ride slowly. It was well he did, for as soon as our boys approached the camp, the biggest dump was blown up.

A huge tongue of flame shot up in the air about 100 feet high, then a mighty crash and showers of dust and debris were scattered all over the place. Sandover told me afterwards that it lifted his Topee, although they were half a mile off.

They rode round the camp and came back to report that it was empty. The Turks did not stop to destroy the remainder of the dump. After this little incident, Lord Hampton told me to ride out and find exactly where the left flank of the Infantry was and the direction they were taking.

Harry Cooks and I rode out to the top of the hill a mile on to have a look round the country. As we watched, we saw what looked like a regiment of cavalry galloping like mad over a rise about three miles away.

Harry and I put it down to a crowd of our wild Australian colleagues on a stunt of their own, but it turned out to be something quite different.

We found the Infantry about two miles away, the left hand regiment was a battalion of the London Scottish. We reported to their Officer, told him where our squadron was and returned. When we could see our chums, we found that they had ridden down into the Turkish camp.

We soon joined them and found that there was a well and stone troughs for the horses. This was Huj, about 8 miles north-east of Gaza. The Turks had broken the pumping machinery and some of the lads were trying to get at the water, others were looking round to see if Jacko had left anything worth having. I joined in the latter group and came across a Quartermasters store tent full of uniforms and equipment.

I got a new nosebag and bucket, and on tipping out a kitbag found a bag of tobacco (about 3 lbs). This was a real bit of luck, for we were very short. It was nearly a fortnight since Allenby's sweep had started. We had all this time been living on bully and biscuits, without extras like tobacco.

There were two or three chickens about and plenty of wood, so we soon had fires going and made the first brew of tea we had tasted in two days.

At about 6.00 pm we mounted and rode off to meet the rest of the regiment. We ran into them just after dark, 4 miles away, and judging by the fires and noise, concluded that the Turks were not in the vicinity.

We were then told to off saddle and put down a line to picket the horses and we realised that we were in for a night's sleep, which we all needed.

Chapter 23

Huj : the glorious charge : After we had settled down, Lord Hampton called us up to him and said that our A and C squadrons, plus one and half squadrons of Warwick's (about 170 men) had made a glorious charge that afternoon and had routed about 2,000 Turks and captured twelve field guns (including three Howitzers 5.9) and ten machine guns. *(See painting by Lady Butler on cover)*

This had broken up the enemy resistance and they were now miles away being pursued by the Australians. Unfortunately we had paid a heavy price for the victory as some good men had gone down including Captain Albright, Lieutenant Edwards, Captain Valentine (Warwick's), Sergeant Farmer Allen, Jim Bunegar and several other friends.

Altogether, 20 were killed and quite a number wounded, including Major W. Wiggin who had a nasty wound on his head which knocked him off his horse 'The Pope' a big strong chestnut. 'The Pope' galloped off with the Turks and was never seen again. This was a loss that Major Wiggin felt very keenly, for Pope was his hunter of pre-war days at Alvechurch and he had been ridden right through the War (3 years).

This news was a great surprise to us all, but I recollected the galloping horsemen I had seen during the afternoon and it was then that I realised that it must have been our pals going for the Turkish guns. We went round to see if particular chums in the other squadrons were alive and well, then we lay down in our blankets behind our horses. Before falling asleep, I thought of our friends who were lying dead, 300 yards away.

How bright and full of life they were that morning. I gave thanks to my Maker for sparing me through the dreadful fight

We had a good sleep and rose at dawn quite fresh. Our first concern was to have a look at the scene of the charge, which was quite close at hand. The guns were standing just where the Austrians had left them, with dead horses and equipment lying around. In the centre of the fight the dead had been collected and covered with blankets. We buried the bodies during the day in one grave.

The temporary cross at Huj

The bodies of the men named below and those of Maj.ffrench-Blake M.C., Pte J.Bond, Cpl J.A.Littlehayes and Pte J.H.Turner killed in other actions were taken to Gaza Cemetery for permanent burial. The nearly illegible names (verified from records) are;

IN MEMORY OF THE OFFICERS , N/C OFFICERS AND MEN OF THE WARWICK AND WORCESTER YEOMANRY WHO FELL CAPTURING THE ENEMY GUNS 8TH NOVEMBER 1917

Maj. T. Albright (Worcs.)   Lieut. S.W. Edwards (Worcs.)

WARWICKSHIRE YEO.	WORCESTERSHIRE YEO.
Sgt G F Plummer	Sgt V. E. Allen
Sgt J. L. Lambert	Sgt A. V. Harrison
Cpl W Kyte	Pte D. Hile
Pte S. W. Sproules	Pte W. N. Griffin
Pte J.W. Bourke	Pte E. W. Bayliss
Pte N. J. Smith	Pte J Bunegar
S/S H. H. Farr	Pte G Mitchell
Sgt J. Pearson	Pte S. A. Perry
Cpl C. J. Shrieve	Pte H. G. Denley(died 9th)
Pte A. H. Adams	Pte R. S. Vickery(died 9th)
Pte W. A. Saul	
Pte E. C. Kendrick	
Pte W. Stacey	

Yeomen buried at Gaza Cemetery, situated one mile N.E. of the Town and only eight miles from HUJ. On or after the 8th November 1917.

Major Ffrench Blake M.C.21st Lancers. Attached Worcs.Yeo		K/A
Major M.C. Albright Worcs.Yeo.Ledbury, Worcs.		K/A
Lieut J.W.Edwards M.C. Worcs Yeo. Coventry		K/A.
Sergt.T.F.Allen	Worcs.Yeo. Worcester.	K/A
Pte A.H.Adams	Warwks. Yeo. ?	K/A
Pte E.W.Bayliss	Worcs. Yeo. Welland	K/A
Pte J.Bond	Worcs.Yeo. Edgbaston	K/A
Pte J.W.Bourne	Warwk.Yeo. ?	K/A
Pte J. Bunegar	Worcs.Yeo. Worcester.	K/A
Pte J.Cooke	Worcs,Yeo. Lye Worcs.	K/A
Pte H.J.Denley	Worcs Yeo. Upton on Severn	K/A
Pte H.H.Farr	Warwks.Yeo. ?	Died
Pte W.N.Griffin	Worcs.Yeo. ?	K/A
Sergt. A.V.Harrison	Worcs.Yeo Dudley Worcs.	K/A
Pte D.Hile	Worcs. Yeo Gloucester	K/A
Pte E.C.Kendrick	Warwks Yeo ?	K/A
Cpl H.Knight	Warwks. Yeo Warwick	K/A
Sergt. L.J.Lambert	Warwks. Yeo. Cropredy	K/A

Cpl. J.Littlehales M.M.	Worcs.Yeo.	Birmingham	K/A
Pte G.H.Mitchell	Worcs.Yeo.	Birmingham	K/A
Sergt. J.E.Pearson M.S.M.	Warwks.Yeo	Tamworth in A.	K/A
Pte S.A.Perry	Worcs.Yeo.	Birmingham	K/A
Sergt. G.F.Plummer	Warwks.Yeo.	Kineton	K/A
Pte W.A.Saul	Warwks.Yeo.	?	K/A
Pte J.N.Smith	Warwks.Yeo.	?	K/A
Cpl. C.J. Shrieve	Warwks. Yeo.	? aet.40	Died
Pte F.W.Spoules	Warwks. Yeo.	?	K/A
Shoesmith W.Stacey	Warwks. Yeo.	Bridgewater	K/A
Pte J.H. Turner	Worcs.Yeo.	Birmingham	K/A
Pte R.B.Vickery	Worcs.Yeo.	?	K/A

Buried elsewhwere; Pte Harold Blackburn Worcs.Yeo see P148.

After breakfast, half the men were sent with two horses to fetch water. They had a very rough journey and were away all day. Those of us who remained got busy and buried the dead horses as they were beginning to get odorous.

We then learnt that the effect of the charge on the Turks had far reaching results. They had formed a rear-guard that was too strong for the 60th Division and their guns were holding up our advance. The business-like fashion in which 200 Yeomen 'set about' 2,000 Turkish Infantrymen, was soon heard about all over Palestine.

The Turks were by this time routed out of their trenches and were at the mercy of our cavalry. The Turkish cavalry never stayed to meet us for they were only mounted on ponies. The consequence of this was that the enemy retreated towards the hills around Jerusalem very rapidly.

They only stayed to hinder our advance when they had the opportunity of picking their position which was usually a good one and put us at a disadvantage.

At midnight, we saddled up and marched north-east through the night. We passed several large villages with plenty of cultivation. We gathered that we had arrived in Palestine proper (at last), after many weary months on the uninhabited desert.

Soon after dawn we reached the Wadi Hesy, an almost dry river (but sufficient water for the horses). After watering we were placed on outpost on some high ground with a good view in front.

I did not quite understand the reason for the outposts, because we knew that the Australians were in front of us. We concluded that our divisions had lost touch with each other owing to the rapid advance, so our Colonel was not taking any risks.

Whatever the official tactics were, I know that we had a wretched day on the look-out. There was a very trying 'Khamseen' wind blowing and we were all tired and fed up; luckily my outpost was near a little village, so we had a plentiful water supply. We amused ourselves by watching the Bedouins, of whom there were hundreds in the valley in front of us.

When we first climbed the hill and looked over, we could not understand what some queer black patches were, but on using our glasses we saw that they were large collections of Bedouin tents. These are woven by hand from dark camel hair and propped up with sticks three or four feet high.

Whole collections of men, women, babies, dog, poultry and other odds and ends, live together in these tents. At night the camels, donkeys, sheep and goats are brought home from their grazing and lie down all round. When the grazing is eaten up in one district, they pack all the tents, pots, kettles, babies etc on the camels, and then march off like an Army on the move.

These are the wonderful Arabs that our poets and song writers tell us about. The famous Arab steeds are generally skinny old crocks that any self-respecting Englishman would not be seen dead with!

We had a fairly good night's sleep here, as far as one can while holding a fidgety horse.

We moved on again in the morning to Arak el Menshize, a large Arab village. Here we halted all day and had a layout on the hill tops round the village to watch the surrounding country. There was plenty of water, so we had a good wash and several cans of tea. Just before dusk, we pushed on a mile or two and set an outpost line across a native road (near Berkusie) to stop all traffic.

12th November 1917: At 3.00 am we formed up and marched towards Ballin, a small village under a hill which commanded a good stretch of country. We sent forward a scouting party, who discovered that this hill was held by the Turks, so an attack was ordered. Our brigade (with a regiment of Australians) had to do this job and a battery of artillery came up at midday to assist.

My troop was left in reserve as escort for the ambulance wagons, along with everyone who was not wanted in the front line. We had a good view of the operations. In fact it was almost a private little fight all to us, without the interference of Generals and Staff Officers. Our boys rode to the foot of the hill, dismounted and attacked on foot. The Turks were few in numbers and bolted as we approached. They retired down the hill to a little railway station in the valley; we learnt that this station was on the Jerusalem to Gaza line. Our lads had not been in possession of the hill for long when a train came puffing into the station and several Turkish Infantrymen jumped out.

The new arrivals, together with the original garrison, easily outnumbered us and forced us off the hill again. We learnt afterwards that we were up against Von Falkenhayn and 5,000 Turks. We stuck to our position until they were a few hundred yards off; we then ran down the hill to the horses, mounted and rode back out of danger. Lord Hampton gave a display of his cool courage in this action.

He was on top of the hill under fire during the whole of the fighting and gave the order to retire when he thought that the Turks were close enough, but he did not retire himself, he remained on the hill in an exposed position watching the Turks coming up to thathim as though they were a flock of sheep that he was interested in.

His orderly, Stan Naylor, who was holding Lord Hampton's horse about 50 yards away on the safe side of the hill, had no sympathy with the Major's study of the Turks. He shouted up the hill "for God's sake come and get on this bl**dy horse".

His Lordship walked slowly down the hill, mounted leisurely and said to Naylor "I shall come down when I am ready and I won't have language like that Naylor".

As they galloped away, the Turks reached the top of the hill and opened fire at them. I wish every Major in the British Army had been as good a soldier as Lord Hampton.

We had 20 casualties in the action at Ballin. Joe Littlehales who was our Sergeant on the draft coming out East, was hit in the stomach and died a few days later, Laurie Dobbs was killed and Teddy Trigg was wounded in the foot. The Brigade was hopelessly outnumbered and nearly surrounded, but luckily for us the Turks did not press that far and they retired towards the Judean hills the following day.

We retired about 4 miles back after dark; we spent the night near a little Arab village, Summiel, where we thought we could get water. However, neither the horses nor ourselves had a drink, so we tied the horses together in bunches and lay behind them and got a few hours rest.

13th November: At dawn we mounted and retired a little into a Wadi, where we stayed all day. Three men from each section were sent out on outpost, but I remained with the horses. We thought that we were a good distance from the enemy, but at dusk we mounted and retired again.

As we rode over some open country the Turks dropped about a dozen shells round us (no one was harmed). We marched about 5 miles in a westerly direction, towards the sea coast, and spent the night near a busy road, which I believe, was the Jerusalem to Gaza track. We managed to get several hours sleep.

At dawn we mounted and rode off to a small Jewish village about three miles away, with the idea of giving the horses a much needed drink. There was a good well here with a pumping engine, but with hundreds of horses to water, the strain on the engine was too great, some of the animals had a drink but our squadron were unlucky and although we waited all day, we did not obtain any water.

The men however were much luckier than the horses, for we managed to buy fresh bread, tobacco, chocolate and even wine from the Jewish villagers. These delicacies were very acceptable, for we had been living very rough for nearly three weeks.

None of us had much money, but I happened to meet Doug Lamb, who was with the Engineers mending the pump, and he was good enough to give me 10/- to get some goods. It was acts like these that proved your pals "on service".

As I said, we did not get water for our horses, so Lord Hampton decided to look elsewhere. Just before dusk, we mounted and rode to Beit Duras, a dirty Arab village about 3 miles away. It was dark when we arrived, so it was decided to wait till daylight, thereupon we tied the horses together and lay down in the village square to get some sleep.

All was quiet for some time but suddenly one dog barked, then his pal and then all of them. I should say that there were 30 of the beasts round about us and they kept up the infernal din practically all night long! We were getting used to the dogs when we noticed that something was irritating us, someone struck a match and we discovered that we were covered with fleas.

The whole of the village square was smothered with fleas and we were all lying down amongst them! We afterwards found out that all Arab villages are infested with the troublesome insects, so we never spent a night in a village again. I shall not forget our night in Beit Duras in a hurry. When daylight came, we found a good well, so the horses soon had their noses in an old stone trough filled with water.

15th November 1917: We re-joined the regiment and heard that Junction Station had been taken the day before by the 75th Division. Also, that the 52nd Division had inflicted a heavy defeat on the Turks near the sea coast.

Junction Station was a big loss to the Turks, because all railway traffic for Jerusalem had to pass through this place and as their main Army had retired to Jerusalem, they were now dependent on a mountain road for the supplies.

At midday we saddled up and marched toward the coast, arriving at the Wadi Sukereir before dark. There was plenty of water in the Wadi so the horses had their fill.

After attending to the horses, a few of us strolled across to a small Arab village (Nebi Yunis, I believe) to see what we could beg or borrow. The Arabs seemed to be destitute, no chickens, eggs or even corn, but after searching the place we found an underground granary filled with tibben and barley.

The Arabs had covered the entrance with bushes, but some sharp lad had found it. There was soon a procession of boys carrying the corn and chaff to the horses, who had a good feed. We were all pleased. It was just as if we had found a store of choice food for ourselves. We enjoyed a good sleep that night.

16th November 1917: Today was spent with everybody having a jolly good bath and washing all the dirty shirts and socks. This sounds as though we all had a portmanteau full of clothes with us, but we all carried a spare shirt and a pair of socks.

We were blessed with a second good night's sleep, so we felt as fit as fiddles. All we wanted was some really good food, for we still existed on bully and biscuits.

17th November 1917: This morning we saddled up and marched across to Tineh Junction. This is where the Gaza line meets the

Beersheba branch. Here the Turks had made huge ammunition dump, no doubt with the view to sending it down in either direction, as required. Apparently they had left Tineh in a hurry, for they left thousands of good shells behind.

We bivouacked here for the night. The following morning, Lord Hampton took our squadron into some hilly country near El Burj for outpost work. Before posting us on our different points, we halted near a large house set in a beautiful garden. We observed some good looking fruit trees bearing a good crop of oranges. Needless to say, we soon scaled the high wall and despite the protests of the native gardeners, we helped ourselves to the luscious fruit. This was our first taste of the Jaffa in its native land and I shall never forget it. One can imagine how delicious the juicy fruit was to us after weeks of bully and biscuits. We learned afterwards, that the house and garden was the country residence of the Greek Patriarch of Jerusalem, so we wished him good luck before leaving. We filled our nosebags with oranges and carried them back to Tineh for our pals in the other squadrons. We spent the day on outpost on the hills round the house. Sergeant Nixon's troop was sent on patrol to ride down a valley about a mile away. When they got there, they were fired on heavily and chased by a large party of Turkish Cavalry. This rather surprised us, as the cavalry had not been seen since Beersheba. We withdrew safely at dusk and returned to **Tineh**, where we remained until dusk the following day.

We now had the duty of escorting the HAC battery of guns. We had just mounted and moved off when rain commenced. It poured incessantly all through that miserable night. The march was not a long one (about 7 or 8 miles), but the night was pitch dark and we had a lot of trouble with the guns. The road was only a track and unfit for wheeled traffic. In fact, it was so bad that whilst passing through an Arab village, the gun that I was riding alongside caught a large boulder and tipped upside down. Righting an 18-pounder gun in the dark, with pouring rain, is no joke. However, we accomplished it and arrived just before dawn at our destination, the famous Junction Station. Here we found large dumps of Turkish arms, equipment and ammunition.

20th November 1917:

There was plenty of wood about, so we soon had a mug of hot tea to cheer us up. We drew rations and rode on at 6.00 am. After leaving Junction Station, we overtook an Infantry Division (the 52nd I think), who was marching up for the attack on Jerusalem. These poor fellows were in their thin 'drill uniforms' and wet through like ourselves. They told us that they had not had a smoke since they left Gaza, ten days back. As we had had two issues since then, we handed out cigarettes to several of them and we realised that even a tired and soaked cavalry man is better than a ditto infantryman. We rode on until we reached Latron, a little place destined to see a lot of our regiment in the days to come. We were told that it derived its name from the Latin, Ladrona (a robber) because it had always been a favourite haunt for highway men. Legend also says that it was called Latron because one of the two robbers/thieves who were crucified with Jesus was born there. It was on the main Jaffa to Jerusalem road, at the spot where the road leaves the flat plain and commences to climb up into the Judean Hills which surround Jerusalem. The Turks held these hills in strong force, yet our lads were pushing them back mile after mile. When we arrived at Latron, shells were bursting on the nearest hills and the infantry were going up towards Jerusalem in large numbers.

The Division which did the bulk of this hill fighting was the 75th, which came from India. It was composed of half Indian troops and half territorial from the west of England who had been sent to India in 1914 when the regular troops were withdrawn. After a halt at Latron, we mounted and moved off up the road to take part in the battle then continue up into the hills. We had not proceeded far however, when a terrific storm came on and the rain fell in lumps. Every horse in the regiment whipped round and refused to face it. After enduring this for some time, we marched on but were turned back and ordered to bivouac for the night as the road was too congested for us to pass. We were not sorry to hear this news, but our next job was how to spend the night on a swamp (it kept raining all night long), so most of us sat on our saddles, which were in the mud, dozed and dreamed of the warm beds we knew in "Blighty".

21st November 1917: Daybreak came at last, but everything was too wet to light a fire, so we had a drink of cold water for breakfast. We then saddled up and moved off up the road, we had great difficulty in getting along for guns and limbers, goods wagons, ambulances etc were all going up towards the troops. We had frequent 'trots' when there was room, this warmed our blood a bit. There was evidence all up the road of the stiff fight that the 75th Division had for possession the previous day. New graves could be seen every few yards by the roadside. During this ride we passed an ambulance, men riding on camels. I saw a fat little man perched on the top of a tall camel. I turned round as I passed him, to laugh, and recognised my old pal Billy Welch, Captain of the GPO swimming club. I had not seen him for many months. Unfortunately, I could not stop for a chat. We kept on climbing this everlasting hill until we reached Enab (8 miles, all uphill). This village was taken by storm (in a fog) the previous evening. Halting on a piece of flat ground by the roadside for a short time, our squadron was sent forward about two miles to Kusteb, where the Turks had destroyed the old bridge over the watercourse.

We spent the afternoon on outpost on a big hill and we were now in the front line with the Infantry, only 5 miles from Jerusalem. We could see a few sheds which were evidently part of the suburbs, but we were disappointed at not having a good view of the Holy City. We were by this time, quite under the impression that our regiment would take part in the final attack.

As we were astride the one and only road, we had good grounds for believing that we were in the position of honour to be 'first in'. However, that was not the case, for at dusk we were relieved by a regiment of the 75th Division and did not see Jerusalem until many weeks later. Just after we had handed over our position, the Turks shelled it heavily and two or three men were killed exactly where we had been sitting all afternoon.

We spent the night at Enab, by the roadside. I remember that the position was bitterly cold, due of course to the altitude (1300 feet). We did however have a sleep on the brushwood, which grew in profusion – somewhat similar to our heather. This was the first sleep we had enjoyed for three nights, so it was very welcome.

22nd November 1917: Our squadron left Enab after our frugal breakfast and we followed a small track across the hills to El Amwas or Emmaus as it is called in the Bible. There is a good sized Monastery here which marks the place where Christ appeared to the two Disciples after his Crucifixion (see St. Luke 24). The Monastery had been turned into a hospital and was full of our men who lay in the rooms, corridors and courtyards, dead and wounded. Fighting was very intensive on the hill just above Nebi Samwil, which was captured by our troops at about midnight. The wounded from this fight were all brought down the valley to the Monastery, where they had their wounds dressed or urgent operations performed. Then they waited their turn to be taken down to the railway by wagon or on camels. The jolly looking old monks were working hard everywhere to assist our RAMC Orderlies, although I was told that a large number of them were German.

Our duty here was to provide gallopers and orderlies for the Infantry Commanders, particularly between Divisional Headquarters and the Brigades, which were scattered amongst the mountains. We picketed our horses by the monastery garden and spent two very restful days. There was plenty of water and wood as it was a nicely sheltered valley – we were warm.
One of our boys, a recruit named Pearson, was sent out with a message late at night and did not return. He took the wrong road and rode quietly into the Turkish Lines. We saw him after the War; he said that he was treated pretty well during captivity.

There are stories of prisoner's treatment in the Regimental library.

23rd November 1917: We were impressed by the wonderful visibility here. It is clear in England after rain, but upon the Judean Hills it was wonderful. Jaffa and the Mediterranean, although 30 miles away, were beautifully clear. The flat country, over which we had been marching and fighting the previous weeks, was spread out like a map before us. However, we were still disappointed in not viewing Jerusalem.

24th November 1917: The hills around Jerusalem were now in our hands. Some rearrangement of the Army was made in order to meet possible attacks by the Turks, also to bring up artillery and supplies of all kinds, for our advance had been so rapid that the supply wagons could not keep us going. We were now about 50 miles from our railway and the heavy rains had turned the dusty plains of a week ago into quagmires. It will be seen therefore that the RASC had a stiff job to contend with. Our main source of supply so far had been camels. But up in the hills these poor beasts died in their hundreds from cold and exposure. A new idea was now introduced. We were amused to see hundreds of donkeys come marching up with our supplies packed on their backs.

They did useful work for some time in the hills, but it was not many weeks before we obtained command of all the roads round Jerusalem. These were put in to good repair, so the motor lorry ousted the donkey from his proud position in the Commissariat department!

We left the old monastery with regret. We marched all day with frequent halts, down the road to Latron and arrived at 6.00 pm. At evening stables, Lieutenant Goodson, newly arrived from England, greeted me as 'Corporal Godrich', this from an old pal with whom I had lived day and night for the first 12 months of the War – I considered that was about the limit! The 'Sam Browns' spoilt Jack Goodson.

25th November 1917: We prowled around and discovered a running brook quite close, so everyone in the regiment had a good scrub down. We also erected our bivouacs and made them as comfortable as possible in case it rained.

26th November 1917: We saddled up early, only carrying arms and food, and went on a 'recce' together with a troop of Warwick's, to the Wadi Surar. The railway from Jerusalem is laid down this valley. As it was about the only possible route that the enemy could use from Jerusalem, we quite expected to come up against their cavalry scouts. However, Johnny Turk was not out that day, so we had a very nice ride round. We visited Artuf, Beit Nettif and Jerash – we searched these villages for Turks or anything that looked suspicious.

The luckiest party on this trip was Alf Gilbert and his section, George Knight, Percy Hodgetts and Hill. They were sent to explore a large house that stood on a hill about 1½ mile away. On arrival they found that it was a monastery. The Monks made them very welcome and insisted on taking them inside where they gave them a good feed and filled them up with wine, besides feeding the horses. They returned laughing merrily but we could not understand the cause of their mirth. No one guessed that they were half drunk because we had not seen such luxuries for weeks. When they dismounted (or rather rolled off their horses) and produced two or three bottles of good red wine, we believed their story and drank to the health of the Monks at Beit Jemal.

We stayed at Latron for a further four days without much to upset the daily routine except visits from Taubes. One of these machines came flying over one day and dropped us a bomb just as we were waiting for some pay. Dick Spencer of 'C' Squadron was wounded. The enemy airman had better luck about half a mile away where he dropped a bomb amongst a crowd of Arabs.

30th November 1917: We pulled down our little houses at last and moved off along the Jaffa Road through El Kubab to a sandy spot between El Mughar and Akir. This was the scene of a good performance by the 6th Mounted Brigade on the 13th November when the Buck's and Dorset Yeomanry charged and captured the position in the face of strong opposition. The Hon Neil Primrose (Lord Roseberry's son) was killed in this fight.
The reason for our move to El Mughar, which was in a westerly direction, was not disclosed to us. Whatever the reason, it was countermanded during the night, for we retraced our steps the following day back to El Kubab on the way to Latron. We halted here for some hours, and then struck north towards the hills. We heard that the Yeomanry Division (which was dismounted) had stood up to some severe attacks from the Turks up in the hills round Tahta and Foka. This was a very important position, for had the Turks forced us back in this direction, they would have cut off all the Infantry who were operating up in the hills round Jerusalem. I heard later that Simpson of the Sherwood Rangers, with whom I was in hospital at Blackburn, was shot at close range by a German Officer. He came from Retford, I believe, and was a good sound pal. Like me he was a Corporal of a Hotchkiss gun.

1st December 1917: The Yeomanry Division had been through a gruelling time up in these hills. We now joined our own division, the Australian, from whom we had been separated, and took over the line that had been held by the Yeomanry Division. I believe this was the last scrap in which the latter took part as a complete division of Yeomanry for they went down the line to re-fit and to wait for reinforcements and were eventually split up. The Dorset's, Stafford's and Middlesex remained in Palestine whilst the others were sent to France in April 1918.

We halted and dismounted in a valley near a village, El Burg. After stripping our saddles of bivouac sheets, blankets and other necessaries, we said goodbye to our horses and the pals who were to look after them. Each man took about four horses besides his own. They rode off south to a camp on the sandy soil near Jaffa. We who were left felt very much as we did when we landed on Gallipoli, only half infantrymen. We quite anticipated a rough time up in these Biblical hills - we were not disappointed.

The first afternoon things began to drag, so to relieve the monotony; Lord Hampton invited Lieutenant Thursfield, a fresh arrival from home, to give the squadron a lecture on the Mills bomb. These interesting little 'lemons' had just been issued to us and all we knew about them was what we had read in the newspapers. Our lecturer did not know much more, or else he was too nervous to tell us. At all events, the only thing I remember about the lecture was that after the bomb burst, it flew into 'chunks'. The lecturer was known as 'Chunky' forever after.

2nd December 1917: We remained in the valley all the following day and we realised that being without horses relieved us of a lot of work.

3rd December 1917: We packed up this morning and marched off to take over a part of the line. The going was terrible; dodging round boulders, slipping up on rocks, climbing steep hills with our rifles and all our belongings was no easy job. When at last we reached the men who were in position, our troop was ordered to relieve a troop of Australians on a little knoll, slightly in advance of the rest of the line, called Walkers Post. To reach this we had to cross about 400 yards of flat area exposed to the Turks who were about ½ mile away.

We did this one at a time, each man being subjected to a very hot sniping on his way across. I felt the bullets singing past my head, but could not run because of my unaccustomed load (also the climb had tired me out). However, we all made the crossing successfully and relieved the 'Dinkums'.

We found this position fairly protected by a wall of large stones that had been built, but we were warned that it was dangerous to show one's head above the wall. We stayed in this position until dawn, when we were relieved by another troop. During the night, half of us were on the qui vive whilst the others slept. To relieve the monotony, I got over the wall and prowled around to see what there was in front. There was a half moon and by its light I found several Turkish corpses. I was just stooping over them to see if they had any souvenirs such as revolvers or field glasses, when two or three shots rang out just behind me and I was startled – they were evidently from the Turks.

A patrol of Turks had probably spotted me silhouetted against the skyline. Before they had time to reload I was well on my way back to our wall. I took the incident as a warning that it was dangerous to rob the dead.

After we were relieved, we crossed the open ground in the half light of early morning without being seen and spent the day in reserve behind a good sized hill. Being rather curious to see the lay of the land, we climbed the hill to look around. Immediately in front of the defence wall was a ghastly sight. Piles of dead Turks in grotesque positions lay scattered around the little hillside. There were about 100 killed in this action that took place in the early morning of 1st December. This was a fresh storming battalion which had been rushed down from Damascus to break our line at all costs (which would cut the Army in two). The positions were only held by a handful of Australian Light Horse (dismounted) but they fought like tigers and were almost overwhelmed by superior numbers, when a company of Scots Fusiliers arrived and turned the tide.

In addition to the 100 killed, 20 wounded were picked up and 112 prisoners taken. All this happened on a front of about 100 yards, most of it in darkness. Amongst the bodies we found dozens of German bombs with handles, the first we had seen.

During the afternoon, as we were lying behind the hill wasting time, a German Taube flew overhead at a fairly good height. He was droning along quietly (apparently having a good look at our front line) when suddenly from nowhere one of our machines dived straight at him. It looked as though he was going to cannon into the German but then he turned and the Taube turned and flew at him. They swooped, dived and turned exactly like two large birds. All the time we could hear the rat-tat-tat of their machine guns firing at each other. They continued like this for about 5 minutes, gradually getting further away until they were lost to our view. It was a very thrilling fight, but I never learnt the ending.

5th December 1917: Today we heard that reinforcements were arriving. At midday we were cheered by the sight of fresh faces and old friends. The majority had come up from Egypt where they had been in hospital. Our old pal, John Mills, who was amongst them, had managed to have a trip home to Blighty.

He amused us when he told us that the day he left home to rejoin us be bought a Daily Mail newspaper and on opening it read that "The campaign season has just commenced again in Palestine and Beersheba has been captured". He said to his friends, "Oh my God, I shall be just in time to be in the thick of it". He was quite right, for about an hour after his arrival an advance was ordered.

We packed our belongings on our backs, climbed over our wall and advanced in open order down the hill towards the enemy. However, we were all surprised at the absence of any opposition. Our objective was the hill on the other side of the valley from where the Turks had been sniping at us. As we climbed its slopes we realised, with much joy, that Johnny had left it to us. We were subjected to a little sniping when we reached the summit, but in those days we did not take much notice of a few spare bullets singing by.

We advanced 1½ miles and found that the Turks had retired to a high ridge running parallel to ours but separated from us by a very deep valley with a small brook running down it. We were now holding the line very thinly as the troops advancing had moved across to the right (or east). This threw more troops into the area round Jerusalem for which we were now concentrating an attack. Up to this point we did a "look out" every alternate night but from now on we were on duty every night. In fact we did four hours on duty and four off, all round the clock. During the daytime we built protective walls, breast high with large stones, as it was impossible to dig trenches. These Sangars, as they were called, were erected about 50 yards apart and were large enough to hold about ten men.

The position was very strong. Although we were few in numbers, the general opinion was that the enemy would soon have their hands full when the infantry started on Jerusalem. Unfortunately for us the rain commenced and it came down in torrents for four days and nights. To say we got wet through is putting it mildly.

We got absolutely sodden, clothes, food, blankets, everything that we possessed got as full of water as it could. We built little houses with stone walls, with a bivouac sheet spread over the top, but the rain came trickling down between the stones. After carefully 'damming' up the stream with mud, a hurricane of wind would blow the sheet off the top. With all this rain, mud and wind, we kept remarkably well. The main trouble with us was that we could not get enough to eat as the rain was filling up the wadis and ravines so the transport wagons were having a difficult time getting through the rivers and seas of mud. The result was that we, up in the hills, were put on short rations.

I remember one little bivouac party consisting of Harold Wood, Alf Gilbert and Champkin These hungry boys made a practice of drawing their rations in the morning, then sitting down and eating the whole lot at once. This was not as greedy as it sounds, I could have done it, but it meant going hungry until the next day (24 hrs) and I was not prepared to practice such long fasts, so I carefully divided my small portions. A few months later, when we were sweltering in the hot sun, we had heaps of food and couldn't look at it. Such is active service.

During one of the storms in the hill, we moved to a fresh position. This meant building new houses. Our Squadron Leader (Lord Hampton) was sitting down discussing plans with other Officers. His servant, Jim Tyler, who was building a bivouac for Lord Hampton, tried to fix the sheet for the roof, but the wind was very troublesome. He fastened down one side and as he went round to fix the other side, up came a fresh gust which blew the whole lot over. This happened two or three times and Tyler became exasperated. He was wet through, cold and tired. Like the ancient inhabitants of these same hills he 'lifted up his voice and cursed'. He cursed the Army, the weather, the Holy Land and everything else that he could think of!

During a lull in the storm, Lord Hampton turned round and said very slowly and calmly "what's the matter Tyler, are you having trouble? Never mind, you shall drive the large car when we get home". I should explain that Tyler was his Lordship's chauffeur in pre-war days. Lord Hampton's remark was heard by most of us round about and the incongruity of it all tickled us to death. We all had a good laugh and forgot the weather. That was how our Major won such a warm place in our hearts.

The worst jobs we had at this time were night listening posts. Two men went out in front of the Sangar towards the enemy (about 200-300 yards), sat on a piece of rock, stared into the darkness and listened. The only thing you could hear was the rain pouring down. Occasionally the monotony was relieved by a pack of jackals. These miserable beasts prowl about all night long and set up the most dismal howl that I have ever heard. There were hundreds of them in the Judean Hills, but we seldom saw one as they hide in holes during the daytime. The English owl's cry is sweet compared to the jackal.

I did a night post with John Mills, the first night after his return from England. John was very depressed of course and he passed the hours away by telling me how well the men at home were doing, he said that miners' strike for more pay and labourers are now earning £4.00 to £6.00 per week, and everybody is making piles of money. Here we were, sitting on top of a hill, cold and wet through, is it any wonder that a soldier sometimes lashes out and hurts the feelings of the men who stayed at home?

9th December 1917 (Sunday): Things were very quiet for a week until we had the news that Jerusalem was taken. We were too far off to hear the fighting, but the news cheered us all up. However, I did a listening post in pouring rain that night which sobered me down again.

ALLENBY ENTERS JERUSALEM
The official entry of Allenby into Jerusalem in 1917, marking the return of the Holy City to Christian dominion. In her 'Housekeeping is Adventure' talk this morning at 10.45, Mrs. Stacy Waddy will describe life in Jerusalem after the War. (Imperial War Museum picture.)

General Allenby forbade any use of artillery against the enemy in or near the Holy City. The whole operation of the Final Assault was made by the Infantry. Those who took part were the 60th Division (London Territorials) and the 53rd Division (Welsh Territorials).

Allenby ordered that no celebrations should be made or flags exhibited.
No mounted cavalry to enter the City.
The mounted man in the picture is a policeman keeping the crowd in order
(Jerusalem, December 1917)

10th December 1917: Our troop went out on patrol over the hills in the neighbourhood. We halted about midday on a large hill. On looking around we discovered a cave which was quite roomy, so we lit a fire with brushes and stood round it to get dry and warm. On arriving back at our old position that night, we were informed that we should probably be taking part in a general attack.

11th December 1917 : During the morning we 'stood to' all ready, but the order to advance was not given, so we played the part of spectators, watching the little Ghurkhas storming the village of Midea which lay about 2 miles away to our left.

We had no further incident of note for another ten days. The rain came down regularly every night, sometimes all day as well. Luckily the hilly nature of the country caused it to run off quickly but naturally everything was soaked through.

My bivouac chum at this time was Percy Hodgetts; he was a brainy little chap and had a brilliant idea one day. We had devised all sorts of drainage methods to keep the rain out of our little house, but to no use. We lay in mud, wrapped in wet blankets at night. Percy suggested a mattress to lie on, I said "oh yes, I'll go along and buy one at Jerusalem!"

But Percy drew his bayonet and cut a pile of thorn bush that grew in profusion on the hills; we then spread it in our bivouac nearly a foot thick, put two blankets on it, and then lay down in our greatcoats with two more blankets over us. We found this an extremely comfortable bed. We occasionally had a thorn come right through, but the water ran under the 'mattress', so we slept high and dry.

22nd December 1917: One wet day followed another with monotonous regularity until the sun came out one morning and we had a warm, fine day. This was the first fine day we had experienced since 4th December, so we were glad to get our clothes off and have a good wash, for we had been fully dressed night and day all this time, which as every soldier knows breeds vermin very quickly. This particular day was a Red Letter day in another respect also, for we actually had an issue of butter, beautiful, tasty, New Zealand butter. It was most acceptable but did not satisfy our hunger for long as we were still very short of rations.

23rd – 24th December 1917: We left our position in front of Kuddis and moved back into reserve, being relieved by the 4th Australian Light Horse. It was fairly fine for our move, but on the 24th (Christmas Eve) it rained in torrents.

Chapter 24

25th December 1917 (Christmas Day): About 10.00am Lord Hampton called a parade, but as we were crawling out of our little shacks, down came the rain again so the parade was cancelled. I had a Christmas greeting from an unexpected quarter. I had taken off my tunic and pushed it into a gap in the wall of our little shanty whilst getting ready to go on parade. I pushed my arm into my sleeve and received a sharp stab. On shaking out the tunic, out fell a large black scorpion that had stung me on my forearm. The sting ached and throbbed all day long and I lost the use of the arm for about 24 hours. I thought to myself, 'this was going to be a Happy Christmas for me'. The rain started again and kept steadily on all day, and to cap everything, when the rations arrived we were informed that only half an issue could be given as some of our wagons were stuck in the mud. I think that this was about the limit for a merry Christmas. Just to round off the 'happy' day, I was the lucky Corporal in charge of the night guard, so did not get much sleep. We remained in reserve on Boxing Day, but on the 27th December we packed up and trekked off to Shuffa in time to take part in the general advance.

The whole line was pushed forward in our sector in order to straighten out for the consolidation that was to follow. There was very little opposition to the advance on our front, but a few miles north of Jerusalem, the Turks did their best not only to stop the 60th Division, but to attack the Holy City. They did not get far.

The day following the advance, we spent in an olive grove where we had a nice fine day of sunshine and in the evening some good fires of olive wood. Two days after, we spent making a road near Dear el Kuddis. This was necessary work for roads, as such, were non-existent up in the hills of Judaea which made the transport of food and ammunition for the fighting men most difficult.

31st December 1917: The general advance ceased. The natives of all the little villages scattered amongst the hills were invited to help with road making, on a wage earning basis of course. The Head man of each village was responsible for a certain part of the road, so he turned out the whole village to help – men, women and children. The result of all this work was very satisfactory, for we soon had a good network of roads from the railway to the front line. Instead of little donkeys, Leyland Lorrie carried rations, stores etc which was a great improvement.

Today we said au revoir to the hills and marched back to El Burj to meet old friends and our horses. Thus this ended a month of hard and tiring infantry work up in the hills of Judaea. We were wet through to our skin for most of the time. We were half starved and physically worn out, but I think I was actually fitter and healthier than at any other period of the war.

I should like to put on record the fine treatment that we received from our Squadron Commander, Lord Hampton, during this trying time. He proved himself a gentleman under difficult conditions, which is the real test.

34 - Hilltop in Judaea – here we spent Christmas 1917. In the distance is one of our shells bursting on the Turkish position

35 - The bridge at Jisr Benet Yacob – broken by the Turks. The water level was much higher when we crossed (1918)

Chapter 25

1918

1st January 1918: We were pleased to see our horses arrive at about 10.00 am and we soon found our saddles and got 'upstairs'. We marched down from the hills and spent the night at Latron. The ground selected for our bivouacs was in a terrible state, soft mud, raining hard, no firewood and very little grub.

The majority of the men spent the night sitting on their saddles which lay in the mud. Jack Mills and I had a walk round the vicinity to see what the other troops in the neighbourhood had to give away. We came across a detachment of Frenchmen and begged a cup of coffee which had just been made – it was delicious and warmed us up considerably. Encouraged by this success, we went on in the darkness and rain and at length came to an empty 'Bell' tent which we at once entered and occupied for the night.

This was a distinct improvement to being seated on a saddle, outside in the rain.

We were up early and made our way back to the horses where we found all our pals wet and miserable. We soon moved off and marched down the Jaffa Road to Ramleh, the sun came out and dried us as we rode along. While passing through the village of El Kubab, a lorry met us and I recognised Bill Miller who was in the Birmingham Post Office in pre-war days. He was a Lieutenant in the REPS, but unfortunately we could not stop for a chat.

There is a very interesting old Tower at Ramleh, which is a landmark for miles around. It is believed to be the remains of a Christian Church founded by the Crusaders.

Years ago Ramleh/ was an important town. At the time of our visit there were still several well built houses.

Now it serves as a halfway rest for travellers on the Jaffa to Jerusalem Road. Lord Roseberry's son, the Hon Neil Primrose was buried at Ramleh. He was killed in the charge of the Bucks Yeomanry at El Mughar. After passing through Ramleh we left the road and went south. It was light and sandy soil and in all directions were vineyards and orchards of oranges, lemons, almonds and figs. We skirted Deiran, a large Jewish colony, and were presented with an orange each as we rode by a large farmhouse. The Brigade Major helped the old Jew to distribute the oranges, we never knew who paid for these and as there were about 800 men in the column, it was a good sized order.

The gift was very much appreciated for it was weeks since we had tasted fruit. We bivouacked that night outside Yebnah, a large and dirty Arab town. We found troughs for the horse's water and plenty of olive trees in the vicinity for firewood – we were 'in clover' compared to the previous night. To complete our comfort, the Christmas canteen issue was distributed. This consisted of a free issue of tobacco, tinned fruit and goods bought with the profits of the Regimental Canteen during the preceding 12 months.

We usually had this on Christmas Day, but owing to the inaccessible position we were in, this had been impossible. The camp fires burnt late that night and we soon forgot our troubles of a few days earlier. We remained at Yebnah for the next day, thoroughly enjoying the rest and making up for lost time by satisfying the huge appetites that we had acquired during our stay in the hill country. The next morning we saddled up and marched off south along the track to Gaza.

This proved to be a rough day's work for we had to cross the low flat country which had been flooded a week or so ago. Every little watercourse had become a roaring torrent; the dusty tracks were now turned into quagmires in which the horses frequently sank in up to their hocks. We crossed the Wadi Sukerier by a new bridge (probably built by the Germans the previous winter). This wadi was a river about 50 yards across and about 10 feet deep, rushing and swirling (this was the little brook by which we had halted last November, absolutely parched with thirst). The only place of any size we passed on the road was Esdud, a large Arab village. We arrived before nightfall outside El Medjel, quite a large town surrounded with gardens and olive orchards. We had a very wet night here, but fortunately were bivouacked on sand, so things were not as bad as they might have been. Our bivouac was quite near the site of Askalon, the principal city of the Philistines. I believe there have been many interesting ruins unearthed here, but we did not take much interest as our main concern was to get a little shelter.

We marched on again the next day via Deir Sineid to Gaza passing much evidence of the Turkish flight of two months before. Mementos such as 12 inch shells, ammunition dumps of various sizes and of course numerous graves were in evidence.

It rained hard all day long. One amusing interlude was when a train of donkeys passed us on their way up to the hills. They were led by Egyptians who were wet through and thoroughly miserable, for these 'sons of sunshine' do not like rain. We did our best to cheer them on their muddy way with facetious remarks.

We halted that night on the old Turkish positions outside Gaza, close by the hills captured by the New Zealanders in the first battle of Gaza. The weather improved for an hour or so allowing us to erect our little bivouacs and attend to the horses, but as darkness fell, the wind rose, the temperature dropped and a violent storm raged all night. In the morning we were out early, but found the horses too stiff and cold to move.

We soon had them off the ropes and coaxed their circulation back before feeding them. After breakfast we marched off again.

We crossed the Wadi Guzze where we had been during the summer of 1917. This, like the others, was full of water and we had wet legs and saddles after wading across.

However, we pushed on and arrived at our destination, Deir el Belah, during the afternoon. The site chosen was in a sheltered spot amongst the sand hills, half a mile from the sea and two miles from the railway station. Bell tents had already been erected for us by a fatigue party, so we soon settled down to an orderly and comfortable camp.

6th January 1918: We arrived at Belah and remained in our comfortable camp for about 3 months of rest and recreation, which did us all a power of good.

The horses needed the rest more than the men for, as Lord Hampton remarked "they look more like scraggy teddy bears than horses". Our saddlery and equipment had also suffered – it was filthy, but this was soon rectified. Cleaning, scrubbing and grooming brought back the polish that had been laid aside whilst the fighting was still in progress. A canteen was commenced, so we were soon living like fighting cocks.

I think our best meal was breakfast; A good plate of porridge with milk from the canteen and a large rasher of bacon with three fried eggs plus bread and marmalade – ample supplies for everyone. The horses were also well looked after in a similar fashion.

After we had been at Belah for a few days, leave to Egypt was announced. I was lucky enough to be on the first party. I travelled with Alf Davis of 'A' Squadron and J. Windram. We left Belah at 6.00 pm and travelled by troop train across the desert to Kantara we arrived at about 6.00 am (a distance of 150 miles).

We then walked across the canal bridge (Suez) to the main line station, caught a fast train at 13.30pm and arrived in Cairo at 17.00 pm. My companions had no knowledge of Cairo, so I took them along to the Metropole Hotel where we were fixed up together in a large bedroom for 22 piastres each for Bed and Breakfast (4s 7d) per night – very reasonable.

Our main occupation during our holiday was visiting different cafes and hotels to compare the food served. This may sound very gluttonous, but I shall not forget the wonderful enjoyment of a bath, a good dinner, a bottle of wine and a clean bed to follow after 'pigging out' in Palestine.

We did not forget our pals and I was pleased to see Harry Scudder again. He was in Nasrieh Hospital recovering from the nasty wound that he received at Beersheba. I took him along with me to see my old friend, Mr Chinn, who entertained us to a nice dinner at his flat. We also visited Harold Blackburn who was in the Citadel Hospital. He had lost an arm in the charge at Huj and was looking very pale and thin. The poor chap never recovered – he died a fortnight later. Harold was a good natured lad. He was on the staff of the Birmingham Gazette before he joined up and his name is borne on the bronze tablet erected in the Gazette offices in Corporation Street.

We visited the Mousky bazaars and made a few purchases. We also spent a pleasant afternoon in the zoological gardens, not only to see the animals, but to enjoy the green turf, beautiful trees and flowers. Our allotted leave was only 6 days, two of which were used up travelling, so we were soon on our way back 'home' to Deir el Belah. We travelled to Kantara where we stayed the night. Bill Shillom and Steve were here also, so I went with them to the famous open air cinema at Kantara.

The troop train did not leave until midday, so we arrived at Belah at midnight. We crawled into an YMCA marquee and slept until the morning. We then walked to our camp having had a wonderful and enjoyable week in 'civilisation'.

The day of our arrival back in camp (Sunday) had been set aside as a Memorial Day for our comrades who had fallen during the operations and a Thanksgiving for our preservation. We had a Brigade Service and, although an entirely optional attendance, quite a large number attended. The Chaplain announced the casualties for the three months as follows:

WORCESTER'S	3 Officers	21 men killed
WARWICK'S	1 Officer	16 men killed
GLOUCESTER'S	2 Officers	12 men killed

Several others died in hospital from wounds received during this period. Having paid our respects to our dead comrades and thanked our Maker for 'bringing us safely to the close of another day', we marched back to camp, had dinner, then proceeded to set about the Gloucester's at Rugby football, both sides were out of training, but we had a good game and won by a try to nil.

The next week commenced with an inspection of our regiment by General Chauvel, an Australian who commanded the mounted troops. Our horses and saddlery were by this time in tip-top condition.

Clipping machines had been obtained and all the horses had been clipped, whilst soap, sand and elbow grease had worked wonders on the leather and steel. Our energies were then turned to drill of all descriptions. Troop drill and riding school in the mornings, then rifle or sword (dismounted) in the afternoons. The Hotchkiss guns were brought out and I had the job of introducing this interesting gun to nearly everyone in the squadron who had not used it.

The weeks rolled by. We even enjoyed the drill for we were well fed and not overworked. We often rode several miles away from camp and spent the morning grazing our horses. Occasionally half a dozen of us obtained permission for a day off and we took sandwiches and rode out to visit the scenes of the fighting of 3 months back. On one of these trips we took a very nice ironwork cross made by the shoeing smiths and erected it over the graves of the men who were killed at Huj. On another occasion, Lieutenant Harvey, Harold Wood and the others took a party of us to the spot where they had cut the Turkish telephone lines 12 months previously. The real tit-bits of our 'holiday' at Belah were two excellent race meetings at Gaza. The course was a good bit of turf situated between the former British and Turkish trenches. The No-mans land of three months ago was now a good steeplechase course complete with 'bookies' on boxes.

The 22nd Yeomanry Brigade organised the first meeting, most of us won a few piasters by backing Major Gooch who steered Clautoi to victory in the big race "The Palestine Grand National".

The second meeting was arranged by the 7th Brigade, but unfortunately rain spoilt the show and the course was very wet and muddy. However, Major Gooch again won the chief event with Clautoi, so we were financially 'high and dry'.

Another Field Day at Belah was our Divisional Sports Day. A varied programme was arranged from jumping etc to smartly turned-out GS wagons. The Australians proved that they were as good in 'spit and polish' parades as they were in the field, as they carried off most of the prizes.

14th March 1918: The whole division was paraded, mounted and polished up to the hilt, for review by the Duke of Connaught, who presented decorations that had been won during the previous fighting. The days slipped happily by, we had occasional rain but were in good tents and on sand that soon soaked it up. My daily occupation was with the Hotchkiss gun and my evenings spent playing cards. My companions at this period were Austin Woodward, Alf Gilbert, Jack Mills and Paddy Hamilton of the 10th Australians. I must not forget Jim Champkin who was a continual source of amusement to us.

On one occasion, after the receipt of a mail from home, Jim was very despondent so we pressed him for the reason and he told us that he had just received a very nasty letter from his fiancée. Some weeks previous, Jim had written two letters home on the same day, one to his fiancée and the other to a lady with whom Jim had a short but very ardent attachment on his last leave.

Unfortunately Jim had put the letters in the wrong envelopes and his real lady friend had resented the mistake!

The last two or three weeks at Belah, were spent in salvage work at Gaza. We rode there in the morning taking cheese and bully and beef for lunch, tied our horses up and occupied ourselves collecting barbed wire, unexploded shells and any spare things we could find on the old battle field. Two large pieces of old iron we did not move were the two tanks that the Turks had knocked out of action in March 1917, they remained on the top of the hill and are probably still there – grim reminders of the terrible fight that raged at Gaza.

Towards the end of March, we were warned that we would shortly be moving up country again. We then received news that our old brigade was to be broken up. The Warwick's were going to France, the Gloucester's to an Indian cavalry division and us to be regimental cavalry to the 20th Infantry Corps.

As far as we were concerned, the news seemed good, for it meant that a number of us would get jobs as orderlies or gallopers to the Infantry Generals but we were sorry to lose our old comrades, most of us had friends in the Warwick's and Gloucester's and the parting was almost as bad as leaving England.

1st April 1918: We marched away from Belah feeling that we were leaving a good home and good pals behind. The Warwick's gave us the opportunity of exchanging any bad or worn out horses for any of their best. They turned out on horseback to cheer us on our way. Many of them rode with us to the Wadi Ghuzze to bid us goodbye. We marched to Ali Muntar on the first day and bivouacked with dozens of British graves all around us.

The plain, around Gaza, was looking beautiful for the Gaza barley was up to the horse's fetlocks and the wild flowers coming into bloom. If anyone contemplates visiting Palestine, let me implore them to see the country in April when the whole landscape is smothered with flowers and the almond and orange trees are in bloom.

The second day brought us to El Medjil, where we had spent a very wet night on our way down to Belah. On the third day we reached the Wadi Sukereir, which was now a quiet little stream, far different from the torrent we crossed in January.

The following day we bivouacked near Deiran in the heart of the fruit growing district. Miles of Jaffa oranges, almonds and apricots stretched out on all sides. These extensive plantations are the result of Jewish colonists work and money.

A visit to the Jaffa district would persuade anyone that if the Jews had possession of their native land, it would again flow with milk and honey. From Deiran we marched through Surafend, where General Allenby's headquarters were situated, past the suburbs of Jaffa to Selmeh about three miles out of town.

5th – 18th April 1918: We remained at Selmah bivouacked on a nice sandy site. During this time we took over our duties as 20th Corps Cavalry, this meant sending numerous men to the 10th, the 53rd and the 60th Divisional Headquarters which were on the Mount of Olives, Jerusalem.

Needless to say, the best men in each squadron were selected and given good horses and equipment. They remained on these jobs as orderlies, gallopers etc until the end of the War. My pal, Austin Woodward, went to the 60th Division and he told me afterwards that he did not regret the move, although the discipline and atmosphere of headquarters was sometimes rather oppressive.

The front line was at this time just beyond Mulebbis, about 8 miles away. We commenced cavalry training in the open. Orders were received announcing that we were shortly to take part in a big cavalry breakthrough, so we were out every day 'sabreing' imaginary Turks.

This was followed by firing practice. During this practice we used some ammunition made in the USA and discovered that 50% of it was useless. It was lucky that we discovered this during our practices or the results could have been disastrous. Naturally we soon picked out the Yankee rubbish and destroyed it - this amounted to thousands of rounds, for nearly all the Hotchkiss gun strips had been loaded with it. This incident reminds me that we were also suspicious of 'bully beef' packed in Chicago for we occasionally came across pieces of sharp wire and bits of tin. I have seen a fish hook embedded in a man's ration.

These may have been accidents, but we put them down to Germans working in Chicago factories. After these incidents, we always demanded the genuine Argentine "Fray Bentos".

During our stay at Selmah we found time to ride into Jaffa sightseeing. The approach to the town from the country is a wonderful sight, the road winds through miles of orange orchards and gardens, the scent of orange is almost overpowering. The town itself was most disappointing, for three-quarters of it was closed and presented a very deserted appearance. I do not know the reason for this. Either the population fled at the approach of the British Army, or perhaps they cleared out while the Turks were in occupation, for they (the Turks) robbed the townspeople of all they could. Jaffa is of course a very ancient town.

It is a maze of narrow winding streets. It is the only port for Jerusalem and southern Palestine and exports oranges and other fruit and imports tourists. Unfortunately there is no harbour, so when the Mediterranean is in a rough mood, landing is very difficult. We also paid a visit to Saronah, the largest Jewish Kibbutz (a settlement) in Palestine. Situated about 2 miles out of Jaffa, Saronah is a beautifully laid out little town and reminded us of pictures we had seen of Los Angeles, although not as 'well off'. The roads are wide with grand avenues of trees.

Most of the houses stand in their own grounds, quite detached from their neighbours. The bulk of the population are German Jews, but the Jewish colonists in Palestine seem to lose their nationality of birth and become Jews of Palestine. We had no trouble at all with the people wherever we went. One and all seemed glad to be free from the 'terrible Turks' who always regarded them as fair game for robbery and oppression. The small bungalow town of Tel Aviv nearby was not worth visiting.

Selmah camp will be remembered chiefly for the oranges that we consumed there from early morning to dark. The camp was besieged by dozens of women and girls selling oranges or exchanging them for bully beef jam or anything else we had to give them. As far as I recollect, the price of oranges was one piaster for a dozen (2½ d) and the main complaint of the troops at Selmah was stomach ache!

Chapter 26

18th April 1918: We left Selmeh and marched to Latron along the main Jerusalem road. We pitched our bivouacs near the road on a rough piece of ground, but after 2 or 3 days, having heard that we should probably stay at this spot all summer, a fresh site was chosen. Bell tents were fetched from the supply depot and we soon fixed up a comfortable camp. We slept in our little bivouacs and used the tents for meals, writing and any other little job that could not be done comfortably in our little shacks. About a mile distant was Amwas, the Emmaus of the New Testament. There was a monastery at this village which had just been vacated by the headquarters staff of the 74th Division. During their stay a very good bathing establishment had been fitted up in the buildings where the monks made their wine. These baths were a treat for us and we made good use of them. I learnt afterwards that this monastery was the place where my friend Chris Thompson of the Birmingham PO was reduced to the ranks for disobeying an order given to him by a fool of an Officer. This took place a week or two before we reached Latron. I should think that this case was unique in Army history. Thompson, who was a Sergeant, was so convinced of the injustice of his punishment, that he appealed to Sir Philip Chetwode, the 20th Corps Commander.

This appeal failed, so he then asked for the papers to be sent to General Allenby, but the Colonel flatly refused to send the case any further.

The GOC eventually saw the case and reviewed it, but also refused to alter the verdict. Thompson then smuggled all his evidence home to England and after a great deal of pressure from his Union, representations were made to the War Office, questions were asked in the House of Commons and the Supreme War Council finally overruled General Allenby and reversed the Court Martial verdict and restored Thompson to his rank of Sergeant with his old seniority.

This process took 12 months and all this time Thompson was bullied and watched by a vindictive Colonel. The mental strain nearly killed him and he had almost become a physical wreck. This is an example of absolute helplessness of a man who is victimised by a bad Officer. Thompson only won by his determination and pluck. Many men would have given in.

I am pleased to say that we never had a case of injustice in our regiment after the departure of the Earl of Dudley in 1915. Later Colonels (Coventry & Williams) were strictly fair and never took much notice of spiteful subalterns or Sergeant Majors unless there was strong corroborative evidence.

Chapter 27

25th April 1918: Cavalry raid on Es Salt, Trans-Jordan: We had only just finished our new camp when we were ordered off on a long journey. The scheme was explained to us as a raid on Es Salt, across the Jordan valley about 60 miles away.

We left our tents standing together with the sick men and poor horses, and marched off up the Jerusalem road to Enab (6 miles, all uphill). We noticed a great change in the temperature up on the hill tops.

We spent the night and the following day in a pretty olive grove. We moved off at sunset towards Jerusalem. Luckily it was a bright moonlit night, so we quite enjoyed our ride. We soon passed the spot where we did an outpost in November last and followed the road, which twists and turns amongst the hills of Judaea.

Between Enab and Jerusalem is a wide valley, this proved a stubborn obstacle for our infantrymen when they advanced on the Holy City, for the Turks had prepared a very strong trench system covering the road (which was eventually stormed by the 60th London Division TA).

The Mayor and his staff walked out of the city and offered the Keys of Jerusalem to a Sergeant, who was in advance of his regiment. Needless to say the Sergeant was embarrassed by the offer and transferred the keys to an Officer.

Reverting to our journey to Jericho, after crossing the valley at Enab, the road climbs up a long hill and we soon found ourselves riding through the suburbs of the famous city.

26th April 1918 (night march): Jerusalem has outgrown its old walls just as Gloucester, Chester, York and most of our own walled cities have done, but the old city is still the heart and core.

The suburb through which the Jaffa road enters is a Jewish settlement. There are many pretty little houses but the general effect is spoilt by nasty little shops on both sides of the road. As we were bound for Jericho, we did not enter the old city, but followed the road outside the wall.

We were surprised to see the wall in very good condition. The Damascus Gate, which we passed, reminded us of old Castle gates, which are still preserved. After passing the Damascus Gate, we were on the Jericho Road which Christ followed many times. The road drops down a deep valley between Jerusalem and the Mount of Olives.

31 The reading of General Allenby's proclamation of martial law
in Jerusalem in December 1917

After passing the tomb of the Virgin Mary and of St. Stephen, who
was stoned to death at this spot, one can see on the hill above the
road, the two buildings which mark the Garden of Gethsemane.
The garden, or olive orchard as it no doubt was, extended all over
the side of the hill, so the Greek and Roman Churches have both
walled off about an acre.

Each built a church, and then they claimed their own spot to be the
actual site. No harm is done by this for nobody knows which is
correct and both gardens are beautifully kept. A little incident
occurred at this spot which shows how callous and indifferent
Army life makes a man.

We were riding in half sections (two's) because the road is not
very wide and my partner, Alf Davis, and I were keenly interested
in everything we saw for the first time. I had been reading about
Jerusalem recently so had a fairly good idea of what the various
buildings were.

My pal, Jack Mills was riding behind me, so knowing that Jack
was a devout Roman Catholic, I turned round in my saddle and
said in a soft voice "this is the Garden of Gethsemane on the left".
Jack said, "Oh is it?" and at once resumed his chat with his partner
by saying "I scooped the 'kitty' with an abundance hand". I
thought to myself, well if that isn't descending from the sublime to
the ridiculous. On the right hand side of the road were the city

walls looking very formidable. Above the walls we could see Church towers, Minarets and other tall buildings, but overshadowing them all was the huge green dome of the Mosque of Omar. It seems incongruous that the largest and stateliest building in the home of Christianity should be a Mohamedan mosque, but that is history.

The road climbs uphill and turns round the shoulder of the Mount of Olives and Jerusalem is lost to view. About a mile further and the quaint little village of Bethany is reached. We halted here at 10.00 pm and rested for an hour, both men and horses snatching a small meal.

We moved on through the village which appeared quite unspoilt by any modern buildings. The solidarity of the old houses impressed us for they looked as if they were built to resist a siege. The windows are up to 8 feet high above the ground, which shows that burglars were fairly common years ago!

After leaving Bethany, the road drops down a steep hill into a valley. The hillside is so steep that the road has been zigzagged about 20 times down the hill. As we reached the top of the hill we could see the long line of horses winding its way right down into the valley. The country now becomes very barren and stony, the olive trees, which grow in great profusion round Jerusalem are entirely absent. We were now approaching the land of desolation and every mile we travelled towards the Jordan seemed more dreary and inhospitable than the last. The distance by road from Jerusalem to Jericho is about 20 miles, but the only human habitation we saw, after leaving Bethany, were two lonely Monasteries.

At the top of one long hill we observed some old ruins and learnt that they were believed to be the remains of the Inn where the Good Samaritan attended to the man from Samaria, who had been attacked by robbers. Even in these times it is not safe to go along this lonely road without protection, for the wild Bedouins still carry on the old game of highway robbery.

We halted at last about ten miles from Jerusalem, having travelled over 20 miles from Enab. We off saddled on a flat piece of ground which was covered with large stones. After pegging down the horses, we had about 4 hours sleep.

At daybreak we were up and took the horses to water, this involved a dangerous climb down into a deep valley where there was a small stream; the path was narrow with the hill on one side and a precipice on the other.

As we took two or three horses each, it can be imagined that the game was not at all funny. This queer spot was named Talaat Ed Dum. At the bottom of the valley we found another pretty little Monastery surrounded by a luxuriant garden through which ran a clear stream of water.

Lower down the valley this stream is diverted into an aqueduct which is cut out of the side of the cliff. This aqueduct, or culvert, is about a yard wide and is cut or built in a wonderful manner for mile after mile along the face of a precipice with a straight drop below.

Who cut it and how it was cut, is not known, but it was done when Jericho was a flourishing city, hundreds of years ago. This little stream supplied it with beautiful cool water down on the desert below. After a few hours at Talaat Ed Dum, we marched on down the old Jericho road. This road is made fairly direct and it is cut down hills that made us sit back on our saddles.

There is a new road to Jericho that is twice the distance, on account of detours to avoid steep hills. The new road is of course used by motor traffic. The old road is worth traversing for the scenery, the prospect of the wide Jordan valley with the Dead Sea, is most impressive. Talaat Ed Dum is 1,000 feet above sea level and Jericho is about 1,000 lower than the sea.

The drop therefore is 2,000 feet in 6 miles. With this tremendous fall everything changes, the air up in the hills is fresh and bracing, but down in the valley, hot and relaxing. The huge barren hills are replaced by a dusty, flat plain which reaches for about 15 miles across to the other side where **the Mountains of Moab** rise steeply to a height of 3,000 feet above the Jordan.

The air is wonderfully clear and we could watch the Turkish cavalry patrols, without glasses, 15 miles away. This all sounds very farfetched, but I can vouch for its veracity.

River Jordan, Water colour by: Lord Hampton

Chapter 28

27th April 1918: We reached **Jericho** at dusk after watering at a little stream; we bivouacked about three miles north of the village. We all had an idea that we should find a good sized town, with some sort of civilisation, but the name of the place flatters it.

I suppose it is well known all over the civilised world and yet it only consists of about 100 dirty little houses and one small Hotel.

The inhabitants are a collection of dirty mongrels - a mixture of Arab, Jewish and European. They scrape a living partly by cultivating small pieces of land by the little streams and partly by trading with, or robbing travellers who are unlucky enough to cross this wilderness between Palestine and Trans-Jordan. The only road across leads through Jericho – it is a halfway halt at which the caravans spend the night.

The ground on which we pitched was very soft and dry, so consequently when we were on the move with horses enormous clouds of dust were created.

This settled on everything, food included, and helped to make our stay unpleasant. It was an extraordinary sight when the horses came back from water, which was about a mile from camp. Every horse and man was covered with fine dust to such an extent that we could hardly recognise each other and black horses seemed to change to brown.

The River Jordan was forbidden to man and horse because of the prevalence of leeches that affected the horses and of bilharzia worms that penetrated the bladders and bowels of humans.

Luckily there was no shortage of water, for several little streams ran down from the mountains and found their way across the plain into the Jordan. The hills of Judaea finish abruptly, and about a mile from our camp was a cliff about 200 feet high. Halfway up this cliff was a strange looking house which seemed to be built on to the cliff. This is a Monastery built to mark the traditional spot where Christ was tempted by the Devil. A small tower at the top of the cliff is supposed to represent the actual site.

One of our wags remarked that if the Devil had shown him the Jordan valley from that spot, he would have told him that it was a rotten hole. There is no doubt that in 1918 this district had to be the most barren place in the World!

It is believed that centuries ago a wonderful system of irrigation made it a veritable Garden of Eden, but now there is no vegetation except alongside the small streams. Everywhere else are little thorn bushes, clumps of deadly nightshade and large boulders which shelter scorpions and snakes (regularly found amongst our saddles and blankets).

At daybreak each morning we had another pest to deal with in the shape of German Taubes, several of which flew over and bombed us. We rolled out of bed and blazed away at them with our rifles, just to let them see that we were about, but no damage was done on either side. During the second afternoon at Jericho, we were called together and the operations that we were to participate in were explained. It appeared that across the Jordan, up in the mountains, was a Turkish Army based on **Es Salt**, a large town about 20 miles from the Jordan.

The Turks were entrenched across the only metalled road which led to Es Salt so an attempt was being made to shift them. The 60th Infantry Division were to attack the position at the front and our division of cavalry were to cross the Jordan, ride north, then climb the mountains along little paths to get round the northern flank of the enemy and, if possible, capture Es Salt thus cutting off their retreat.

While this was being done, the Hedjaz Arabs had promised to attack the southern end of the Turkish position – thus hoping to squeeze them into submission.

We marched off at dusk, leaving our bivouacs and all spare equipment in the care of several sick men - Jim Champkin was the representative for our troop. At about 9.00 pm we reached the Jordan and found a swiftly running river about 30 yards across. A pontoon bridge had been built and we crossed without incident. We pushed on through a thick growth of tall grass and reeds and after travelling about 5 miles dismounted and lay down by our horses waiting for dawn.

We were now close to the Turks. As soon as daylight came, firing commenced. It did not seem very severe and we soon discovered that it came from the Turkish outposts on the little hills above us. We mounted and rode along the level for a mile or two, taking no notice of the odd bullet.

However, one of these found its mark and Sergeant Turk of the Gloucester Yeomanry was killed. Turk was a great sportsman, always in everything strenuous. He was also very bald which made him the butt of many jokes.

We came to an opening in the hills and left the Jordan valley and followed a track up into the mountains, which was so narrow and steep that we had to dismount and pull our horses up after us. We climbed up hour after hour and every time we topped a rise, the Turks had a shot at us.

Occasionally a troop was sent to dislodge a Turkish Post about half a mile away but they never stayed to fight. We soon discovered that they belonged to the Caucasian Cavalry and although they looked very well mounted, they never allowed us to get near enough to measure swords.

About midday we struck a shepherds hut right amongst the mountains. A well close by provided men and horses with a welcome drink. We had climbed about 2,000 feet during the morning and the change of air was very refreshing. We had several lengthy halts, but eventually reached an open valley near Es Salt at dusk.

Conflicting reports came through about our success but orders were given that no lights or fires were to be shown. Strict economy with rations was also ordered. We carried 3 days supplies but as we were more than a day's march from a depot with several days work ahead, we looked like going hungry.

We had a poor night's rest and were glad when dawn came. We soon had fires alight and cans of tea made. We had scarcely finished our tea and bully when we were ordered to parade dismounted and wearing shrapnel helmets.

We handed over the horses to a few men and set off towards Es Salt with Colonel Williams stepping out ahead. One of the Australian regiments had entered the town the night before but had to clear out owing to the large numbers of the enemy still in occupation. An attack on the town was now being made from three sides. We pushed on quite expecting a rough house from the garrison. However, when we reached the top of the hill looking down into the streets, we could see that they were deserted – the birds had flown, for which we were much obliged. A messenger was sent back for the horses.

We mounted and rode down into one of the quaintest old places I have ever seen. Es Salt has a population of about 4,000 people, mostly Christians. It consists of very sturdy stone houses and several Churches. It is built on the side of a steep ravine, down which flows a good stream of water. Alongside this stream are gardens and orchards of olives and figs. It is therefore an extremely pretty little spot, especially after a stay at desolation like Jericho. We had now reached our objective and our next task was to dislodge the Turkish Army which lay between us, Jericho and 'Home sweet Home'. Es Salt itself was quite empty of Turks, although 24 hours before it was the headquarters of the 4th Turkish Army. We now turned west towards Jericho and after marching about four miles, turned into an olive orchard where we off saddled.

The road ran alongside a brook so we were soon cleaning off the dust and dirt of the last two weeks. Our big problem now was food, for the hard work up in these mountains had increased our appetites and heaven only knew where tomorrow's grub was coming from. The food question was solved by purchasing sheep from local Arabs. We carried a good supply of tea and sugar and as there was plenty of wood about and a good stream close by, we had frequent brews. Late in the afternoon, we saddled up and climbed a big hill about a mile away.

We decided that this was Tel um Allah, approximately 2,500 feet above the Jordan. We put our horses in a sheltered spot near the summit and spent the night on outpost. It was bitterly cold and heavy clouds rolled over us all night long, so we got very wet!

2nd May 1918: Soon after dawn, we were withdrawn and returned down the mountain to the olive grove. We had a small breakfast and then ordered to prepare for a dismounted attack.

The horses were left in charge of a few men, but we led sufficient horses to carry the Hotchkiss guns. The plan of campaign was that we were to attack simultaneously with the Infantry.

The latter troops were on the other side of the Turks, pushing up the Es Salt road – we were advancing down the road. It was hoped to force the enemy out of their position by double pressure.

36 - Australian Mounted troops in Es Salt in Judaean Hills

Although there were nearly two divisions of cavalry at Es Salt, all these troops were not available for the attack. The main body was engaged to the north of the town holding off the enemy who had been rushed down the Hedjaz railway to Amman and were now trying hard to recapture **Es Salt.**

If this attack had succeeded, more than half of Allenby's cavalry would have been captured for there was only one way out for us. Owing to the determined attack, only our brigade could be spared to co-operate down the road with the infantry.

As we could not all occupy the road at the same time, the Worcester's were ordered to deploy over the hills on the eastern side, whilst the Gloucester's did the same on the west - the road being left to our artillery, which was a battery of small guns carried by mules.

We scrambled up and down hills for several miles, getting tired out in the process, until we reached a wide open valley with a steep hill about 200 feet high on the far side. This hill, named El Howej, was our objective.

We started to cross the valley when suddenly a battery of 5.9 guns opened on us with high explosive. The noise was ear splitting and we soon discovered that the shooting was also very accurate. A bunch of three men at once drew a shell or two and we soon had some casualties.

We took what cover we could find behind the boulders and kept on towards the hill. Our little mountain guns opened fire but they were not powerful enough to reach the Turkish guns. We tried to work our way through the trees and tall grass by the little brook, but the shells followed us everywhere.

Captain Mitchell, Lieutenant Burton, Corporal 'ginger' Richardson and Sergeant Major Brunson stopped for a minute and were stood together chatting, when a shell dropped amongst them and killed the first three. Billy Brunson was knocked over but unhurt. Dicky Bird of 'C' Squadron, who came out from England just three weeks before this 'stunt' was sitting behind a large boulder, when a shell dropped and blew his arm off!

This artillery activity was quite unexpected to us. We still had a considerable distance to go before we could use our rifles and it became apparent to us that we should lose half our strength before we struck a blow (we were only about 200 strong) – we were up against a big proposition.

We advanced again towards the hill but the shelling became so hot and furious that the Colonel at last ordered a retreat. We were all very glad to get the order, for we felt we were trying to do the impossible.

Our way home was up the valley to the road instead of over the hills by the way we had come. The Gloucester's on the other side of the road had fared no better than we did and retreated also.

I was one of the last off the scene of butchery, having stayed behind to help the stretcher bearers etc and I almost lost my life. Coming quietly up the valley I came across Bert Siddaway of 'A' Squadron who said that he had spotted a sniper who was firing at the stretcher parties. I said "right, we'll snipe him".

We lay down together, Bert with the rifle and I with the glasses, giving him his distance etc. We only had two shots at the sniper when a shell burst right over us.

My first thought was that we were both killed, but then I realised that I was alright and after the dust and smoke had disappeared, I turned to my pal and asked him if he was okay. Unfortunately, he was hit in the back just above the kidneys and could not walk a step. We were in a quandary, all alone with everyone clearing off as fast as they could go. The road was about half a mile away, up a rough slope. I dashed off up the slope and managed to get a stretcher and 2 helpers, together we carried Bert to safety.

It was hard work for us as he was a six-footer and weighed 13 stone. I am glad to say that he recovered and got home to England. This incident taught me a lesson that I shall never forget, 'if you have the chance to clear out of trouble, clear out at once and don't hang about'.

We struggled back up the road to Es Salt in two's and three's, talking things over. We learnt that the 60th Division, who attacked the other side of the Turkish position, had been driven back and instead of us having the Turks squeezed between two forces, it now looked as if we should probably be squeezed.

We reached the bivouac where we left the horses absolutely dead beat, but were soon heartened by a good brew of tea that had been prepared by that thoughtful little chap Billie Shillom. Darkness came on and we were soon wrapped in our blankets and fast asleep. The next day, at dawn, we were visited by Taubes and they continued to bomb us merrily all day long. However, they did no damage to our regiment for we remained in our olive grove well hidden. Towards dusk we had the order to saddle up and prepare to move.

We dumped all our spare ammunition in the river, lit up big fires with olive branches and moved off quietly at about 8.00 pm. We had a very rough night march, on foot most of the time leading our horses, for our way lay right across the mountains along narrow goat tracks.

We walked on in single file, hour after hour wondering if the guide knew the way and quite expecting to come up against a Turkish outpost. Nothing happened until about 2.00 am when we halted on a piece of flat ground up in the hills, large enough for us to form up the whole brigade.

We stayed here till just before dawn. The Brigadier gave orders that we should keep steadily on, there was to be no bustling or excitement. We were to expect an attack, but with luck should all get back to the Jordan safely.

This was good advice, for soon afterwards the sun rose and with it came four Taubes. These cursed machines chivvied and worried us for miles and miles, dropping all their bombs on us, then peppered us with machine guns. Whilst this was going on we were picking our way carefully up and down steep rough hills, such as the Alpine club might choose for a holiday resort.

We kept steadily on, we could see the Turks closing in all round us but luckily they were about two miles away, so did us no harm. One or two horses lost their footing and fell down the hill sides, but otherwise we managed very well and at about 10.00 am we emerged at last on to the flat ground of the Jordan valley. We breathed a sigh of relief at this and considered that we were all out of a very nasty corner.

I found myself riding next to Alf Gilbert and as we went quietly along towards the Jordan Bridge, Alf said, "what date is it?" After referring to my diary, I said, "4th May", he said "I thought it was, it's my birthday", I said "many happy returns", "thanks, it's the first time I have celebrated it like this!"

Bridge leading up to Es Salt

We crossed the river and reached our bivouac near Jericho at about 1.00 pm – horses and men quite done up. Es Salt is about 20 miles from Jericho, but we had made a wide detour because the Turks were entrenched across the road which connects the two towns. The distance we had covered therefore, was probably about 30 miles, mostly on foot, up and down rough mountain paths. No wonder we were tired. We were surprised to learn that Jim Champkin and the other sick men whom we left behind in camp, had been called out in our absence to help fight off a large body of Turks who tried to capture the Jordan Bridge.

If this attack had succeeded, two complete cavalry divisions and one infantry division would have fallen into Turkish hands. However, the 4th and 11th Australian Light Horse, assisted by all the men that could be scraped together, put up a stubborn fight and held the bridge for us. The only losses were eight guns of the HAC and Notts batteries – no men were captured.

EsSalt did not fall until Brig. General Wilson C.B.,C.M.G.,D.S.O., Croix de Guerre, attacked the town with a large force of Australian Mounted troops. The 3rd Brigade of Light Horse rode into the town on 1st May 1918 and continued up the road to Damascus capturing over11,000 prisoners.

Chapter 29

5ᵗʰ May 1918 (my birthday) : Today we did nothing except attend to the horses. Many of the poor animals were lame, through hurting their legs or feet against the sharp rocks we had clambered over. We remained at Jericho until 10ᵗʰ May when we packed up and marched uphill to Talaat ed Dum, about 10 miles distant. It was very hot at this time in the Jordan valley, so we marched after sunset. We returned up the new road, which we found more roundabout than the steep old road down which we had come, but it was much easier for the horses. We spent the following day at Dum and marched the next night to Enab (21 miles) via Jerusalem.

We passed through Bethany and Jericho on the march, but there was no moon this time, so we did not see much of either place. After a day at Enab, we marched to our old camp at Latron (10 miles). It was like reaching home after being abroad and we all felt very much at ease in our nicely laid out little camp.

We arrived back at Latron on 12ᵗʰ May and did not move again until 31ˢᵗ July. Looking back at this long stretch, I have only happy memories of Latron.

Our food was plentiful and good, our regimental canteen was well stocked with all the extras that a man wants, the discipline was easy and the duties were light. In fact we almost forgot that there was a War going on.

(Lord Hampton's water colours convey a good impression of the countryside at Latron).See Appendix.

It was 90 degrees in the shade every day, there was nothing going on along the whole front in Palestine – operations commenced each year in September.

We had official telegrams and papers from home telling us of the peculiar happenings in France in March and April. We read of the Germans capturing town after town and then we were told that 'strong counter attacks had been made, inflicting severe losses on the enemy'.

The news gathered was conflicting and it was not until we reached England and talked to the men who were there, did we realise how nearly the Germans came to winning the war in March 1918. However, as we were blissfully unaware of this serious state of affairs, we did not worry much. Our little War seemed to be progressing very well. Our mornings were usually spent in mounted work, troop drill, sword drill or exercise rides. Dr. Teichman gave us a course of first aid work, demonstrating how to get a wounded man on to horseback etc.

The midday meal was a light one, the cooks only making tea. The afternoons were spent in listening to lectures, Hotchkiss gun instruction, kit or arms inspections. Hot cooked dinner at 5.00 pm and the evening playing cards completed the day. The surrounding district was very interesting, so we frequently formed small parties and went for a ride.

We had sham fights - a favourite for these was the little village of Abu Shushe which stood on some high ground about 3 miles from camp. We captured this place dozens of times in different ways. The villagers responded to these attacks by invading our camp, but in a peaceful way. They came with dozens with oranges, tomatoes, melons and similar things and they did a thriving trade for everyone was glad to buy a few extras. Eggs or tomatoes for breakfast, grapes or melons for lunch were the order of the day!

One day I was approached by Captain Jenner who was in command of our squadron during the absence of Lord Hampton who was on leave.

He asked if I would go up to the front line to instruct some infantrymen in the use of the Hotchkiss gun. I thought this would give me an opportunity to see something new, so I accepted. I packed up and left the regiment on the 22nd May with orders to report to the 53rd Division Headquarters.

I got a lorry at Latron dump and travelled to Ramallah, a small town about 8 miles north of Jerusalem on the Damascus Road. This was a very interesting trip. I knew the road well as far as Jerusalem, but it seemed much more pleasant on a joy-ride than when marching to Es Salt with the regiment.

The lorry was one of a convoy which made the journey daily, part of our wonderful system for feeding front line troops up in the mountains of Judaea.

The supplies came by sea to Jaffa, then by train to Junction Station or Ludd. They were then carried to Latron near our camp and from there they were sent to divisional dumps 20 miles away by a fleet of lorries. The trip to Ramallah was about 30 miles, over some very big hills, about 3 miles north of Jerusalem.

I was interested to see Nebi Samwil, the hill that cost the 74th Division many valuable lives in the December fighting. It was crowned by a small building in white stone, reputed to be the Tomb of the Prophet Samuel.

On arrival at Ramallah I reported to O/C dump, who was a Major of the RASC, a fat gluttonous individual. He looked as though a month with the infantry would do him good. When I asked him to provide me with a conveyance to take my gun and myself to Divisional Headquarters, he ordered me to clear out as he was 'too busy to attend to trivial matters'. I expect he wanted his tea, so I thought I would see what I could find. After wandering around a little, I struck the 60th Division HQ and soon found two pals, Sid Lane and Fred Taylor, who were orderlies from our regiment.

They made me welcome and I had a good meal and a comfortable night with them. After breakfast and a wash and shave, I strolled across at 10.00 am to see the fat Major again. As soon as I appeared he said "Ah, here you are, where the devil have you been?"

I reminded him of our previous interview, but he said he did not remember. It transpired that his divisional headquarters had been wiring him for me and he had the 'wind up' because he knew that he had sent me off and did not know where I was.

He was a nasty man, a bully and there were many of them in the Army, most of them in soft jobs.

After the interview I was found a Ford car and we were soon bumping our way over a rough mountain road to the 53rd Division HQ. The headquarters camp was in a pretty little valley near Ain Sinia, on the main road. After reporting to the senior staff officer, who treated me like a gentleman, I was given a guide.

We left the main road and struck into the heart of the hills for El Taiyibe, a little village on a hill. I had at last arrived at the 53rd Divisional Cyclists, whom I had to teach all about the Hotchkiss gun. The Cyclists were a merry little contingent, about 50 strong, hailing mostly from Cheshire. They soon made me feel at home. Their Commanding Officer, Captain Derry, gave me a hearty welcome, then handed me over to his two Lieutenants, Holyoake and Stern, with whom I spent the first day talking over the Hotchkiss gun and mapping out my course of instruction. The next morning I unpacked my gun and started with my first class and a second class in the afternoon.

After tea, I went for a walk with Corporal Harrison to the village of El Taiyibe, where we found a very interesting old Christian Church. The old Priest, who looked more like a Monk, showed us around the little building with great pride.

Unfortunately he could not speak English, so my bad French was the only means of communication. However, we made ourselves understood and I remember that he seemed disappointed when he learned that we were not Roman Catholics.

We had two more days at Taiyibeh with lessons in the morning and afternoon. We then packed up and marched forward to Kefr Malik, in the front line.

We pitched our bivouacs on a hill from which we could see miles ahead, range after range of rough Judean hills as far as the eye could reach. It looked impossible country for troops to capture and I could not help wondering how on earth we were going to turn the Turks out of it. However, this was done three months later.

We made our little bivvies very comfortable with the aid of the large stones which were scattered everywhere, but the Hotchkiss gun lessons were badly interrupted because the Cyclists now had to take their share of front line duties and after the men had been out all night putting up barbed wire or on listening posts, they were more inclined to sleep during the day.

However, I kept at it and was now taking three classes a day. This lasted for about a week when Lieutenant Stern and I went for a walk and found a quiet little valley which we thought suitable for a shooting range.

We fixed up some rough targets and the next day the whole company took out lunch and we spent the day firing. The gun went very well, much to my delight, for machine guns have a nasty knack of going wrong when you need them most.

The day after the firing, the new guns arrived for the Cyclists so I spent the day examining them and making out a list of shortages etc. Although it was June, this was a very cold job, for there was an extremely cold wind blowing. I could not help comparing the temperature with that at Latron, which goes to show what a difference elevation makes to the weather conditions.

This was my last day with the Cyclists. I had been with them for 12 days and taught about 30 men how to handle the Hotchkiss gun, so considered my time well spent. I had a good report from their OC so presume that he was satisfied. I was given a fatigue party to carry my gun and my kit and we walked to the 159th Brigade dump near Tel Asur where I boarded a lorry which took me to Ramallah, the home of the fat Major. I did not trouble him on my return but went across to see Sid Lane again who soon fixed me up with food and drink. I spent a night at Ramallah and found another lorry next day which carried me to Latron. The camp was just as I had left it and the boys were glad to see me back again. I soon noticed the change of temperature and sighed for the cool breezes that I had been enjoying during the past fortnight up in the hills.

The campaigning season was approaching and the Colonel wanted every man to know something of the Hotchkiss gun. I was given another beginners class of 10 men, some keen, some indifferent and some lazy. I did my best to tell all I knew. Whilst we were doing this the others were put on bombing instruction when a funny incident occurred. Our Troop Officer, Lieutenant Lindsay, occasionally lapsed into broad Scots jargon which we did not understand. One afternoon he had our troop out with bombs. John Mills was sent forward with two other men to a little trench from where they were to throw three live bombs each. John threw his bombs away at once, got out of the trench and came quietly back to the troop (he hated the sight of bombs). Lieutenant Lindsay could see that he had not thrown his bombs properly and called out "what do ye wish Corporal Mills"? Meaning of course, "what are you coming back for?" John pretended that he didn't understand and said very gloomily "what do I wish; I wish this bloody War was over".

Around this time, George Knight and a few others obtained leave and left for England. This was their first trip home for 3 years. On his return, George was a married man! A Church Service was fixed up at the Monastery at Latron so a party of us walked over on Sunday mornings for Communion. This seems rather a trivial remark now, but at the time such a Service was an event for those of us who participated, for we were without a Padre and were very rarely near anywhere to join in a Service. Day after day rolled by, the heat increased and our little camp was now quite unlike the pretty green patch when we first arrived in April. Not a blade of grass existed and clouds of dust rose from the slightest breath of wind or movement of men and horses.

We had a useful canteen established and it was presided over by Bert Millard, assisted by George Powell (who came from

Blackwell). On one occasion Bert made his usual trip to Ludd for his supplies but found that there was a serious shortage of beer. He knew that the troops could not go without a drink so he thought that he would give us a treat and bought several small barrels of wine made at Richon near Jaffa. It had been a very hot day and everybody had a fearful thirst to quench after the sun had gone down.

The Richon wine was cheap and good, the run on the canteen was extraordinary, so much so that by 'lights out' more than half the regiment were merry and bright. Bert Millard bought wine again the next day and the result was the same – the fact being that the wine was too 'heady' for us. Colonel Williams prohibited wine again and I think he was probably right for the weak beer suited us much better. We never forgot the two 'wine nights' at Latron when even abstentious men fell victim to Bacchus.

One day in July we had bad news, for it was given out that our Doctor was leaving the regiment. Captain Teichman, who had been with us since mobilisation, was extremely popular.

He was a brave man who had 'dressed' men under heavy fire on numerous occasions. We knew that he did not feel very much at home with our new officers and after Toby Albright was killed at Huj, he seemed a very lonely man – he and Toby were great chums. Dr Teichman attended several of our reunions after the War.On one of these occasions he presented me with a copy of his book 'Diary of a Yeomanry Medical Officer'.

(See Regimental Library at Worcester)

We had 3 or 4 Doctors afterwards, but unfortunately at the time of our greatest need during the big push to Damascus, we had an old Italian Army doctor who was drunk most of the time and whilst he was with us, we lost 25 of the best men in the regiment from Malaria and other diseases. I am not alone in thinking that had Dr. Teichman

remained with us many of these valuable lives would have been saved. I know that Jack Hemming, the poultice wallah (dispenser) thought so.

The month of July dragged slowly on, each day seeming hotter than the previous one. Towards the end of the month, three days leave, to look around Jerusalem, was announced. I applied for a Pass but unfortunately before my turn came I developed boils on my knee. They were very painful and prevented me from riding and I walked with difficulty. My trip to the Holy Land was therefore cancelled. Before the boils were cured, the regiment had orders to proceed to the Jordan Valley to take part in outpost and patrol work. The fearful heat in the valley was causing a lot of sickness and many soldiers were being carried off to hospital with sunstroke and fever.

Finally, the regiment packed up and marched off on 31st July 1918. I was left behind with the sick and lazy and my knee did not show any improvement. Our doctor had left with the regiment so I had to visit a neighbouring unit about a mile away. This walk, over rough ground every day, did not improve matters and finally I could not walk at all.

On 12th August an ambulance collected me and I was taken to a casualty clearing station at Ludd. On the 14th August I was taken with a large party of sick and wounded, put on board a hospital train and sent down the line to Kantara Hospital. I remained there for a week, during which time I had several boils lanced. Things did not improve however, and finally I was sent to Cairo where I reached the 27th General Hospital at Abbasis.

A smart young Doctor examined my knee and pronounced it patella bursitis or fluid on the knee. He operated the following day and cleared it out. The wound healed rapidly and I was soon hobbling around.

There was also a good Dentist in the hospital, so I took the opportunity of having my teeth put right and was made a new man. Whilst in hospital I had a welcome visit from Harry Scudder and Stevenson. The first day I went out I met Norman Brodie who was in Cairo on leave. He told me that he was off back to Jerusalem to join the regiment as there was a big stunt commencing shortly. We little imagined then that it was the last great stunt that broke the Turkish Army into a disorganised rout.

The next week was spent in Abbasia convalescent depot in the old infantry barracks. I found Jimmy Windram here and together we went across to see Harry Scudder who was now in the Labour Corps as a B2 man (Harry was badly wounded at Ras el Narg). Windram and I also went into Cairo to look round the bazaars. We spent one afternoon with Doug Lamb, Bert Crosbee and others who were in the Citadel Hospital.

Chapter 30

19th September 1918: Today we received our marching orders and were packed off to Cairo Station and took the train to Kantara. The main topic of conversation now was whether we should be in time for the stunt, also how far we should push the Turks. I remember that I was rather pessimistic after our two fruitless raids on Es Salt and the hill country north of Jerusalem. I considered that 20 or 30 miles would be about the limit. I thought we should probably get as far as Damascus in 1919 or 1920. We all thought the War would go on for many more years!

We arrived at Kantara at 3.00 pm and on reaching the Yeomanry camp learnt that the 'great stunt' had commenced at daybreak. Most of us were as keen as mustard to get to our regiments and I soon found the camp orderly room and persuaded them to put us on draft at once. We spent one night at Kantara, then left on the 'Desert Express' at 2.30 pm, passed Gaza at midnight and arrived at Ludd at 6.00 am very tired and dirty. 200 miles in a cattle truck in 16 hours is an ordeal. If you don't believe me, try it yourself.

We remained for one day in the 20th Corps details camp near Ludd Station. We were then to march to Jerusalem on foot, 30 miles mostly uphill. I almost gave up, but it was too late to turn back and could only hope that we should do it in easy stages. This turned out to be correct, the first day we did 8 miles to Latron. We marched along at a very comfortable pace, but most of us had come straight from hospital so were very soft and unfit. We found a little camp waiting for us just across the little brook from our old camp where we had spent such a pleasant summer. The old site was deserted, for the men and horses which I left when I went to hospital, had moved to Jerusalem. Windram and I looked across at the old horse lines and somehow the old camp site reminded us of Goldsmith's *Deserted Village*, for we had spent many happy hours at Latron.

The next day we marched 10 miles to Enab up in the hills. We had a day's rest at Enab then set off on the last 10 miles to Jerusalem.

The hill air was invigorating and we were getting fitter – we actually burst into song on this trip. The Jerusalem camp was on the Bethlehem road, with a wonderful view of the city in front of us. I found out where the Worcestershire camp was and soon made my way across to it. SQMS Jack Mills was OC details here.

It was well situated about mid-way between Jerusalem and Bethlehem with a fine view of both. These two famous cities are only 6 miles apart, so were within easy walking distance of the camp. Bethlehem women visited us in large numbers with oranges, grapes, eggs etc for sale. I was very struck with how good looking many of the girls were. They seemed to be a superior type to the average Arab woman one sees in Palestine.

I learnt that Bethlehem is practically a Christian town whereas Jerusalem is mostly Muslim or Jewish. The natives of these large towns were in a very bad way when our troops captured them and they were glad to get hold of our money for anything they could tempt us with.

In the early days of occupation, one regiment of Australians seemed to have an inexhaustible supply of money so the natives did a roaring trade with them. The Egyptian notes that we had were unfamiliar to the Jerusalem fold, so some smart lad thought of using the labels from Ideal Milk tins.

The word 'Ideal' was printed in red and gold and when carefully cut out, the label looked very important. Dozens of these labels were passed off on the natives of the Holy City before the game was discovered. The English papers called us the modern crusaders who delivered the Holy City from the hands of the unbeliever!

27th – 29th September 1918: I spent three days in our little camp at Jerusalem. I managed to have a good look round the famous places outside the city walls, viz: Gordon's Calvary, Gethsemane, Valley of Jehoshophat, St. Stephen's Gate, Virgin Mary's Tomb and others.

Unfortunately I did not find time for a close look at the interesting buildings inside the city walls. On the fourth day after our arrival at Jerusalem, about 20 of us were fixed up with horses and kit. Harry Talbot and myself were put in joint command and told to proceed to Ramallah, 17 miles north, where we should find Lieutenant Matthews and a draft of remount horses, which we were to take up to the regiment. Nobody knew where the regiment was except that they were on the road to Damascus (190 miles away).

30th September 1918: We left Jerusalem by the Damascus Road and marched 17 miles to Ramallah where we found Lieutenant Matthews. Soon after our arrival, a party of Australians rode up with about 40 horses. We had no ropes, pegs or any other appliances to tie them up, but we managed to find a small garden with a good wall round it. This kept these wild remounts together during the night. The next morning we were busy for we had 60 horses on our hands and only 20 men to look after them.

This would have been 3 horses each, but unfortunately we had 2 or 3 men, Sergeants, Farriers, Armourers etc. who would not do their share, so this threw more work on the others. Our main trouble was carrying the corn, luckily we had spare saddles and these were loaded with nosebags full of corn for the spare horses.

As we proceeded on our march, we came across the debris of the battles that had just taken place and managed to pick up ropes, pegs, sacks etc which helped to lighten our task of looking after such a large number of horses.

1st October 1918: Our second day's march was from Ramallah to Khan Labon, 20 miles. Khan Labon was in a sheltered valley just behind the old Turkish front line. There was a pretty good water supply and judging by the empty shell cases, old tents etc., it had been an important place with the Turks. On this march we crossed what had been no-man's land during the previous six months.

It was interesting to observe the difference between our well-made roads and those of the Turks. The old front lines were well defined by barbed wire, but in place of trenches, stone breastworks were used by both sides.

The fighting had not been very severe on the Damascus Road, so we did not see the ghastly sights that were so much in evidence around Gaza a year before. The Turks in this part of the line fell back rapidly, owing to the fact that our cavalry (who broke through 30 miles away near the sea coast) got right round to their rear. The Turks fell back 12 miles to Nablus in Samaria.

Our regiment, which was the first to travel along the road, met with no opposition until we neared the town.

2nd October 1918: The third day we travelled from Khan Labon to Balata, a village near Nablus (12 miles). We found a small dump and a few men and horses belonging to our regiment. We heard a lot of news – first that Damascus was captured on the 1st October. This surprised us for it was about 100 miles north; none of us thought that men or horses could do such a distance in such a short time. The next item of news was that **our regiment had made a charge** at the very spot on which we were now bivouacked. It appeared that the Turks hurried out of their front line, made for **Nablus** (situated in a large valley) and left a rear guard at the village of **Balata** to cover the entrance to the valley.

Our boys were suddenly fired at from the village and our CO decided to gallop straight at them. This was done, but unfortunately the Turks had posted themselves on the flat tops of the houses and could not be reached.

One or two machine guns commenced rattling and saddles were being emptied, so 'retire' was sounded and our boys galloped away to cover. They dismounted and advanced on foot – the Turks took to their heels. One man was killed and about half a dozen wounded.

This fight took place around Jacob's Well and the little Church built nearby. The town of Nablus is the ancient city of **Shechem** in Samaria. This well, which is now surmounted by a stone cupola and looks very dignified, is reputed to be (and probably is) the well mentioned in the Bible, where Jesus asked the women of Samaria to give him a drink. We bivouacked nearby and without bothering to do any exploring, had a quiet night's sleep. One couldn't help but think of the events that had taken place at that very spot, as recorded by St. John (Chapter IV).

3rd and 4th October 1918: Before we left Balata, we decided to have a look at the **Wadi Fara** about which we had heard rumours. The Wadi is a small river running swiftly from the high plateau of Samaria down to the Jordan, about 200 feet below. A road ran alongside the river with high cliffs on one side and a steep drop on the other. We learnt that the Turks retreating from Jerusalem had chosen this road to escape from our Army who were on their heels, rather than continue on the main road to the north.

Their Officers made a bad mistake because they forgot that the British Air Force was out looking for targets. The retreating wagons etc were spotted and the head of the column was bombed, which blocked the narrow road before it reached the Jordan valley where it would have been safe.

The whole column built up nose to tail down the steep and narrow road not knowing what had happened and unable to turn round or reverse. The Air Force acted quickly – relays of planes from Ludd rained bombs on the helpless occupants of the vehicles which stretched for about five miles. It was a scene of destruction that I shall never forget. As far as the eye could see, the human bodies had been removed and buried, the animals had merely been tipped over the side into the swift stream where they lay stinking.

Chapter 31

5th October 1918: We travelled on our way through the town of Nablus (Shechem) on to Sebustie (Samaria) to the important centre of **Jenin**, a trek of 30 miles through a very hilly district. Jenin was an important Turkish Army Camp for stores of food and fodder, all captured by the Australians.

6th October 1918: Having filled our nosebags and haversacks, we travelled on from Jenin to **El Afule**, a road and rail junction on the plain of **Esdralon**. This small town was previously the centre of several Jewish settlements, but the Turks had made it a centre for reserve troops and stores etc. When we arrived it was obvious that the local natives had enjoyed looting everything moveable.

7th October 1918: From El Afule we climbed up the hills to **Nazareth**, a distance of eight miles. This small town is nicely situated in a depression surrounded by hills which give it a sheltered appearance. Mount Tabor (1800 feet) is only six miles from Nazareth.

Seen from a distance as we approached, one could only see the buildings perched on the high ground, the most prominent of these is the Casa Nova, a hospice built by the Roman Catholic Church for the benefit of pilgrims to the Holy places. There are four Churches: R.C., Protestant, Greek and Greek Catholic plus a Mosque. Apart from these and a French college, we thought

Nazareth was a grubby Arab town. We stayed only long enough to give our horses a drink, and then moved on to **Kefrkenna**, Biblical **Cana in Galilee**.

We bivouacked under the olive trees near the famous spring which bubbles out of the rock. Kenna is only a village, but we strolled around and found a few Arab girls who could speak English (educated at an American Mission in Nazareth). They invited us to their home where we found the whole of the family engaged in making lace or crochet work.

After a cup of coffee and a chat, we were of course invited to buy some of their work to take or send home. Unfortunately we had not been paid for some weeks so we could not buy much. I took their names and addresses and had several orders sent to them after the War which the family of Saffoori faithfully carried out.

Before we left Nazareth, which I did not see again, I must relate an episode which occurred soon after the great breakthrough of 19th September. The 5th Cavalry Division rode through the gap in the trenches which had been breached by the infantry at 7.00 am and rode steadily north without meeting much opposition, all through the day and the next night.

One Brigade of the Division, consisting of Gloucester Yeomanry and two Indian regiments under the command of Brigadier J. V. Kelly, was sent on in advance towards Nazareth with the object of surprising and capturing the German General, Von Sanders, and his staff.

The Brigade covered 45 miles in 22 hours, a remarkable performance, but owing to some delay in dealing with a few Turks in a village near Nazareth, the alarm was given, the German sentries and guards were alerted and in the confusion and darkness, Von Sanders and his Officers escaped in fast cars by the Damascus Road to the north.

Read' The Last Crusade' by Anthony Bruce

General Allenby was furious that this well planned raid had failed and Brigadier Kelly was removed from his command. We met him riding south some days later, he was looking very sick and sorry, we did not know the reason until a few days later.

8th October 1918: From Kefrkenna we trekked steadily on to **Tiberias**, a small town on the lakeside of Galilee. En-route we passed two prominent little hills which seemed to stand as sentries to a flat grassy piece of land of about 20 acres. The hills are known as the **Horns of Hattin**, the grassy plan is reputed to be the scene of the last battle between the crusaders from Europe and the Arabs or Moors from North Africa.

This battle ended the attempt by Christians to recapture the Holy Places of Palestine (AD 1187). The Crusades from Europe took place mostly in the 12th Century. The Mohammedan rule held the Holy Land until we, the British Army led by General Allenby, drove the Turks out eight centuries later! Another little legend about this spot near the Horns of Hattin is that this was the very place where Christ fed the 5,000 people who had been listening to him. To continue on our journey we descended from the high land near Hattin (about 800 feet above sea level), down a series of zigzags to the lakeside which is nearly 700 feet below sea level – a drop of 1,500 feet in approx. 2 miles.

Approaching Galilee from this altitude one is disappointed with the smallness of the scene. The clearness of the air adds to the apparent size of the little lake. It is pear-shaped, only 14 miles from north to south and only 6 miles across from east to west, although it widens out to 8 miles further north. The Jordan runs into the lake at the north and out at the south so that the water is always moving which kept it fresh. *(See Lord Hampton's watercolours)*

We put up our bivouacs about a mile from Tiberias right on the lakeside, enjoyed a swim and watered our horses which were covered with dust. Before turning in we chatted for hours on the great events recorded in the Bible which might have occurred at that very spot.

There was some argument about the great storm that wrecked Peter's boat until our Lord stilled the waters, but it was agreed that the lake is probably liable to sudden gusts of wind sweeping down from the high land which would be strong enough to jeopardise a small fishing boat.

Chapter 32

9th **October 1918:** Up early for another swim in Galilee, saddle up and another interesting ride along the lakeside for about 10 miles where we halted to have a look at the ruins of ancient **Capernaum,** nothing but stone pillars and blocks. We thought it strange that not a sign of human habitation had we seen since leaving Tiberias. From Capernaum the road turns north into the hills where we found a cosy little Jewish settlement called Rosh Pinnar which is two miles from the Arab town of **Safed**, perched on the top of a hill. Many of these old towns are built on hills, chiefly because they were liable to attacks by bandits in the old days. The Turks were more subtle in their robbery, the head man of the village was taxed on the number of families under his control and he had to find the tax or else! St. Matthew was a Tax Collector under the Romans.

We found a good many Jewish settlements (Kibbutz) like Rosh Pinnar throughout Palestine; they live on a communal basis, no individual purse, and agricultural work for man and women.

The people I met were all from central Europe, the majority German, all very friendly and all delighted to be free from the Turkish overlords. Plenty of fruit and eggs available here and cheap enough to suit our pockets, a tin of bully beef was good enough for a bucket full of oranges.

10th October 1918: From Rosh Pinnar the road turns north-east and crosses the Jordan. At this point there was an ancient stone bridge (Roman) called Jisr Benat Yakub **Jacob's Bridge** (see p144) but the Turks had destroyed the central arch in their retreat to Damascus, so the only way of crossing the river was by fording. Before we tackled this awkward crossing with four horses each and in view of a long ride the following day, we decided to bivouac for the night.

11th October 1918: We were up early and started off down the steep and stony bank urging our horses across the swiftly running river. The horses stumbled over large boulders with the water up to their bellies and to our stirrups – but we got across without incident and climbed the steep bank and were away up the road to Damascus. Our journey that day took us through hilly country, not very interesting, to the town of **Kuneitra** (about 18 miles). The natives were very suspicious of us, as we were of them. We learnt afterwards that Kuneitra was a town populated by Circassians and very pro-Turk.

Circassian women are reputed to be the most handsome in Turkey, but we did not see any – no doubt shut in to avoid being molested by wicked British troops.

During the march we saw the great mass of **Mount Hermon**, 30 miles way. We could not understand the patches of white on its side until someone suggested that it might be snow. Later we found a map of Hermon which gives the height as 9,200 feet, this surprised us but explained the snow and the manner in which Mount Hermon dominates to landscape for miles around. I was riding with Frank Townsend on this trip.

I think it was he who suggested that the mountain might be Hermon and he quoted a Psalm to me (Psalm 80) "Tabor and Hermon shall rejoice in thy name". Frank had been a choirboy and man at his village Church so knew his psalms, pre-war he had been a huntsman with the Croome Hounds.

Following this line of enquiry in Psalm 42, which has the well-known verse: *"As panteth the hart after the water brook......., I shall remember thee from the land of Jordan and the Hermonites".* Also in Psalm 133: *"As the dew of Hermon and as the dew that descended upon the Mountains of Zion".* All of which proves that the Jews of the Ancient World were quite familiar with this magnificent mountain - a most impressive sight. We posted guards at Kuneitra that night in case the locals took a fancy to our horses or saddles, but the night passed without incident.

12th October 1918: We marched on from **Kuneitra** on the Damascus Road and soon ran into the dustiest and desolate country we had seen since the Jordan valley, absolutely barren, no vegetation – nothing but volcanic dust and boulders. We were now only 15 miles from Hermon which reminded me of Fujiyama and other extinct volcanoes.

This awful country we were travelling in was obviously made up of lava thrown out by Hermon many centuries ago. We covered 16 miles and halted at a small Arab town, completely walled in, named **Susa**. A fresh stream ran by the town which was handy for watering the horses and a good wash down for the men.

Chapter 33

13th October 1918: Our final day on trek, we left Susa early and marched 18 miles to arrive at **Damascus** at 5.00 pm (185 miles from Jerusalem). The only item of interest on the road was a huge crowd of Turkish prisoners guarded by Australians. I rode across to one of the Aussies and found to my delight that it was Paddy Hamilton of the 19th Light Horse. Paddy and I had been great friends at Gaza and other places whenever our two regiments had been near each other.

Paddy told me that they had about 10,000 Turks in their charge but they were too weak to run away and that many of them were dying from cholera, exhaustion etc. At that I thought that we should be moving off, so I trotted on and soon caught up with the others.

Damascus: The first sight of this famous city from high land is astonishing. It is a large city consisting of flat roofed Arab style houses packed closely together, with many Mosques pointing their dainty minarets towards heaven. The most astonishing sight is the green belt surrounding it.

This belt consists of orchards of olives, figs, pomegranates, oranges etc., with gardens which grow melons, green salads and vegetables all year round. Water is abundant everywhere, some of the city streets have fresh water running down the gutters.

This is due to the proximity of two fast running streams (the Abana and the Pharpar) which are mentioned in the Bible (Kings II.5). Naaman thought they were preferable to the Jordan for bathing. Anyone who has seen the rivers would agree with Naaman. Modern names for the rivers are Abarna and Barada.

We soon came across our regiment who were camped under some olive trees. They had the task of looking after about 3,000 Turks and a house full of German Officers, several of whom seemed to despise everyone else, British or Turk. No guarding was required, all the poor Turks needed was food.

They had no hope of getting anything if they went down to the city unless they were Syrians, but the majority of the Turkish army was genuine Turks from Anatolia which was many miles distant.

14th October 1918: Our first task was to parade with the 60 horses that we had brought, all safe and sound. This was easy because volunteers had been asked for amongst the prisoners, and we all had one or two Turks waiting on us like slaves and enjoying better food and conditions than they had in the compound or in the Turkish army.

The horses were walked round in a large circle while Officers in the centre chose horses for their respective squadrons. I was leading an Australian mare, not much to look at but I had ridden her several times on our long journey and had decided that she was my horse for the remainder of the War; she was one of the most comfortable rides that I ever had.

She had a sensitive mouth, 'capable of being ridden on a silken thread', as the old horsemen used to say. Unfortunately for me, Major Mayden who was a regular Officer serving with us knew a good horse – that is how I lost my favourite. As the days went by, the help given to us by the Turks became more valuable because an increasing number of our men went sick and were sent to Hospital. A virulent type of malaria had broken out.

We learnt later that many of the cases originated at Beisan where the regiment had stayed for 2 nights at the foot of the hills surrounding Nazareth on marshy ground which breeds a nasty type of malaria carried by mosquito. Our pals were taken off to Hospital on the outskirts of Damascus where we visited them occasionally taking them what presents we could find (chiefly fruit and cakes).

When we first visited the hospital we found a 3-storey stone built block which looked more like a barracks. Inside we found it most repulsive, overcrowded, dirty floors, army blankets which did not look clean, no sheets and a general air of despondency over it all.

The only nursing staff that I saw, on several visits were German orderlies, the equivalent of our RAMC who took very little interest in their patients. I was visiting some of my friends on one occasion when a German orderly came round the ward with a hypodermic giving all and sundry a jab.

After each injection he took out of his tunic a dirty rag and wiped the needle (shades of Lister and Co!). No wonder our men died like flies. Our regiment history tells us we lost 31 men at Damascus; many of them sailed from Avonmouth in April 1915 and had been through the whole campaign.

Friends who died in this horrible hospital were SQMS Ben Barnett, a very old Yeoman who was over 50 years of age, Harry Cooks of

Kings Norton, Reg Fearn from Erdington, George Powell of Blackwell and John Bull of Worcester.

We took them one by one to a Christian Cemetery on the north side of the city; a Padre read the service over their graves. We had wooden crosses made by a native carpenter and we erected them over their graves.

Harry Cooks' grave north of Damascus, with comrades. Note the Field Ambulances in the background. This picture was presented by the family of Corporal Rowley who went on the charge at Huj armed only with his signalling flags.

There is no doubt that the strenuous days of the weeks before we reached Damascus caused debilitation that could not withstand an attack of malaria. We carried on with our daily duties of guarding prisoners who did not need guarding. One bright relief came when some trucks arrived to take them away. We were glad to be rid of the arrogant Germans.

Portrait of Victor Godrich by German P.O.W.

13th October – 20th November 1918: During this time whilst still at Damascus we heard various reports of the progress of the Indian Army Cavalry to the north and their capture of the important towns of Homs and Hama. We also heard of a hold-up at the city of **Aleppo** which is 200 miles from Damascus.

The Turks tried to prevent our troops reaching the important Railway Junction of **Muslimie**, where the valley to Mesopotamia branches off, but they gave way on 28th October. This surrender isolated their Army at Baghdad and the important oil fields.

We learnt afterwards, that while these battles were being fought, the Allies in Greece were beating the Bulgarians who were suing for peace. Defeat on the west and east convinced the Turks that it was all over.

Chapter 34

Armistice signed on 30th October 1918: Looking back over the years, I cannot remember any elation or rejoicing over the news of the Turkish surrender, probably because many of us were ill and very tired.

39 - Damascus Avenue, designed by the French

189

40 - The Railway station with the Syrian Military Band
A postcard photo taken before the Occupation by British Forces.

Vue de Damas et Salakie

A French postcard showing the turning place *for the horse drawn*
gharries taken before the occupation of Damascus. .

Chapter 35

PEACE AT LAST

We still had the use of our horses, so were able to do some exploring of the old city. We found the street called **straight** where St. Paul lodged. We saw the meaning of 'Straight' which is 'narrow'. Riding round the old streets we could not help wondering at what marvellous events had occurred in Damascus over its long existence. The advantage obtained by the city was due to a large extent to two beautiful streams of fresh water that had for centuries given life and prosperity to a city set in a vast area of barren land.

Towards the end of November, several of us developed malaria. This had decimated the regiment but instead of being hospitalised in the 'black hole of Damascus' as we called the place where our comrades died, it was decided to evacuate all sick men by rail to Palestine where there were Field Hospitals. This was made possible by the British engineers who had repaired the railway that had been destroyed by the retreating Turks.

We were taken by truck to **Damascus** railway station, a well built place, where we boarded a train and travelled south on the famous Hedjaz railway – which was destroyed by Colonel Lawrence and his Arabs. The train took us to **Dera'a** Junction where we had to change to a narrow gauge which went in a westerly direction down to the Jordan Valley. The line twisted and turned down the gorge of a small river, which runs into Galilee, a drop of 2,400 feet in 30 miles.

A change of trains and we arrived at **Ludd** (Lydda), where we found Harry Scudder and other friends who soon provided everything needed. The regiment arrived with the horses; some saddles were occupied by Turkish POWs who had volunteered to do the journey. A few days later we heard that we were to spend Christmas in Cairo!

3rd December 1918: Men and horses entrained and travelled down to **Kantara** in a few hours, with a recollection that it had taken us 2 years to reach Ludd travelling in the opposite direction. Ludd to Kantara (on the Suez Canal) is approximately 200 miles.

We entrained on the western side of the canal in Egyptian State railway coaches and reached **Helmia**, near Cairo, where we found a tented camp in a pleasant situation. After attending to our horses, our duties were light except for restoring horses, saddlery, equipment and ourselves to a more civilised condition than we had been in during the previous six months. One special occasion is remembered. General Allenby, whom we all admired, expressed a wish to see the regiment on parade. We all accepted the honour with pleasure. Needless to say, horses and men were on their best behaviour that day.

There was a NAAFI canteen near the camp where we could spend an evening playing cards or listening to a few singers, but our chief delight was to walk into the city and find a clean restaurant for a good meal and a drink. The return journey to camp could be made by a gharry holding 3 or 4 rowdy soldiers, pulled by a poor old horse who was half dead, there was also a much cheaper method which was to hire a donkey with the owner running by his side, the rider sat on the donkey's rump without saddle – a precarious position after a few drinks.

We soon found that Army pay did not allow many such outings because prices had risen since our stay in Alexandria three years before. I have a record of one memorable trip to the city with a few friends. We had tea at **Ezbekia** by the Nile followed by a visit to the Kursaal to enjoy a performance of 'Miss Hook of Holland'.

26th December 1918 (Christmas Day): We celebrated in the time honoured manner. We sat down at 4.00 pm, but I have no recollection of the time that we retired to our tents. This was the first time that we had been able to enjoy Christmas since the hospital occasion at King's Lynn 4 years previously. We remembered Christmas Day 1917 when we were cold and wet through on the Judaean Hills.

1919

The regiment remained at Cairo until January when we entrained again and returned to **Ludd**. This was a sensible move because we were sending men into hospital daily with signs of Asian flu which was sweeping through Europe at the time. Some of our comrades who were left behind did not recover and were buried in Cairo.

We reached Ludd in a pleasant camp amongst olive trees, but we discovered that we were soon to march again, this time it was across the Jordan to **Amman**, the Arab town that we had tried (without success) to capture a year previously. We packed our saddles and rode off on our peaceful mission.

This time to prevent our Arab allies fighting each other. Jerusalem was reached and we halted for the night near the railway station. Next day down the long hill to **Jericho**, 15 miles and 2,000 feet drop. We spent one night there then we crossed the Jordan and climbed **the hills of Moab**.

From Jericho to Es Salt (24 miles) we recognised the place where we spent three dangerous days the previous year. On to Amman the next day – a total trek of nearly 90 miles from Ludd, and further away from home than we expected to be when we were at Cairo. We were now on the high plateau of Trans-Jordan; the air was fresh, the weather good and rations plentiful, so we forgot our troubles at Damascus and Cairo and enjoyed ourselves. Lord Hampton was our CO. He was more interested in Roman ruins and other antiquities than in disciplining his troops.

Our duties consisted of visiting Arab villages and Bedouin tribes in order to 'show the flag' (as the Navy called it) or to let the Arabs see that the British Army was still in the land that the Turks had vacated, also as a side line to stop any tribal fighting that might take place. This suited our Major because it involved visiting villages of historical interest. We all welcomed the change of a few days in a new area and Lord Hampton made the outings interesting by telling us the history of the country.

All good things come to an end, and I was called to the orderly room (a tent occupied by Sergeant Major Norman Brodie) to be informed that my group (civil servants) was listed for demobilisation. This was a sad blow because I felt fit and well, enjoying myself with rides into unknown country. I had a chat with Brodie and told him that I had no desire to go home yet, on the other hand I knew that there were other men from the GPO in a similar group to me. I had nearly 14 years seniority on my PO rank and at a thousand miles distance, Birmingham seemed very inviting.

There was also the fear that if the other men of my group returned before me, I might have been disciplined, so I chose to go home. I shall never forget the night before I left. Tears were very close but the Quartermaster, Bill Walker, produced a jar of rum and we forgot our sadness, someone remembered a few ribald songs and we crept to our tents at peace with the World.

This was the end of my Service with the Queen's Own Worcestershire Hussars with whom I had served on active service since 6th August 1914. I was discharged from the Army on 3rd May 1919.

F/M Allenby displays his troops in a march through Aleppo Mar.1919.

Chapter 36

Homeward Bound

The journey home from Amman was interesting so I should like to recall a few events that occurred during my long journey.

Two or three other men were due for demobilisation, so we rode off to Regimental Headquarters which was to **Serafend**, near Jaffa, a distance of about 90 miles. Our main risk was the thieving Arabs for whom we had to keep a sharp lookout, especially at night, but we arrived without loss, said goodbye to our horses, obtained our passes and boarded a train for Kantara some 200 miles distant, on the Suez Canal.

25th February 1919: At Kantara we found hundreds of men of all regiments, eager to get home and resume 'civvy' life. We spent three weeks in the demob camp (as it was called) waiting for our group number to be called.

On 18th March my number was reached and we left Kantara by train to Port Said. We then sailed away from the Land of the Pharaohs or other names given to it by soldiers that may not be recorded here.

We were under the impression that we were bound for 'Blighty' but we learnt from the crew that our ship was taking us as far as Taranto (the southern tip of Italy). Three days later we entered a fine harbour, disembarked and spent the next three days exploring Brindisi and the country round about which we found to be uninteresting.

The camp was well equipped with cook house, sleeping quarters, baths and a barber's shop plus a good canteen. There was very little discipline so orders became requests that everyone obeyed. Rifles had been left behind in Egypt; all we had to bother with was our kit bags and greatcoats.

A few of us who were cavalry men managed to smuggle our swords away which we were taking home as souvenirs. We marched to the railway station where we found a train of cattle trucks waiting for us!

26th March 1919: Everyone who has travelled in France will be familiar with the legend "12 Chevaux – 20 Hommes". We were privileged passengers so were packed only 12 to a truck which gave us ample room for sleeping and moving about. Blankets were plentiful, but in southern Italy in March the temperature was kind.

The journey from Brindisi to Le Havre was slow but very enjoyable. Our train was not given any preference which meant that we were run into a siding when overtaken by a fast passenger train. This generally occurred near a town where we had time to nip out for a "vino" or fruit to quench our thirst, or to buy something unusual. As we travelled on we noted the names of places we passed. The first stop was Taranto, then to Bari and other seaside towns.

Those of us who remembered our geography realised that we were travelling along the shores of the Adriatic and that we should not see anything of Naples or Rome on the western side – very disappointing. Another memory was the improvement in the countryside, vineyards and cultivation instead of the barren land of the south. The natives seemed to be better dressed and the women folk more attractive.

We had an hour or two at Rimini, time for a walk round this famous old city. Our next stop was inland at Farli where we found a rest camp with warm baths and a hot meal waiting for us – this was our third day of travelling so was very welcome. We left Farli in the evening and enjoyed a good night's sleep, waking to find that we had bypassed Milan and were nearing Torino (Turin) – departing from there later that day. As darkness fell we were glad to make use of our spare blankets because we knew we were nearing the Alps. We passed through Mt Cenis tunnel during the night and arrived at a rest camp at Chambery in the French Alps.

31st March 1919: Warm water for washing and shaving but no hot meal. There was a café nearby where one could buy café au lait and a snack. A fat and friendly French woman behind the bar who kept calling out as each one entered "fermez la porte, s'il vous plait", those of us already there helped Madame by shouting the command at everyone else. As there was a cold wind blowing from the snow clad Alps all around, a warm café was important.

On down beautiful scenery through Aix les Bains to Lyons, a large city situated at the junction of the Rivers Saone and Rhone, both of which were in flood. Further on we pulled into a siding and found a well-equipped rest camp, a hot meal and plenty of cheap wine. We crept under the blankets at peace with the world and had a good night's sleep.

We awoke to find we were in Le Havre where we exited the cattle trucks which had been our home for over 6 days. We had a hot meal and baths on the cliffs at Harfleur. We sailed away from France during the evening, landing at Southampton late at night.

We entrained at once and woke to find ourselves in a lonely camp on the Wiltshire Downs (Fovant). Our journey from Kantara had taken us nearly 3 weeks (8th March – 5th April).

5th April 1919: Fovant was one of the demobilisation depots for troops arriving from overseas. Looking around we saw several regimental badges cut out in the chalk hills indicating that various regiments had camped here during the war.

We also found that the camp was enclosed by a high barbed wire fence, the entrance gates guarded by sentries. The whole place resembled a POW camp inside and outside. The treatment we received from the smart young men who inspected, examined and searched us old soldiers was both annoying and humiliating, but we were all anxious to get home and a protest or argument might have caused some delay.In the first shed our Army pay books were taken from us and a few pounds given to help us home. There was a collecting box placed in a prominent position!

My medical inspection was a success. The MO tested pulse etc and enquired if I had contracted any disease. I informed him that I had suffered from enteric fever and malaria to which I was still prone. This was entered in my medical record and much to my surprise I was awarded a disability pension of 10/- weekly which I enjoyed for 2 years.

The final order to take all kit bags to a shed depressed us. We had to suffer the indignity of tipping out the contents for inspection by the youthful staff. Many of us had brought home souvenirs and presents, all of which were scrutinised. Excess army clothing was removed. The item of my souvenirs that I thought the searchers might fancy was an Arab knife with an inlaid shell handle which I hid down the leg of my trousers.

6th April 1919 (Sunday): We left Fovant 'POW camp' in the morning and arrived at Snow Hill station where I said *au-revoir* to several friends, caught a tram to Sparkhill, walked with my kit bag on my shoulder to 32 Wilton Road. I knocked at the door and was welcomed home.

Here is the end of my journey from Amman, Trans-Jordan.My army leave expired on Saturday 3rd May. I reported for duty at the GPO Birmingham on 5th May which was my 32nd birthday.

This diary was written between 1920 and 1930

APPENDIX 1

watercolors by Lord Hampton done in Palestine 1916-19 while on active service.

These paintings can be seen at the city Museum at Worcester

144   Marakeb December 1916

164   Sheikh's tomb above Amwas Judaea

003   Brigade H Q at Tel el Fara early morning

151   Sea of Galilee Jordan valley

151   Jordan Valley & River

Mountain of Moab across the Dead Sea

129   **Bivouac at Bir Abba**

004   **Poplar trees at Latron June 1918**

005 Latron olive plantation.June 1918 Farm is other side of hill

163   River Jordan Winter 1918

161 Latron after end of war. June 1918

201

160   Latron View from Abu Shusheh Judaean Hills afar.

158   Judaean Hills   June 1918

159   Judaean Hills and Transjordan June 1918

157   Judaea and Transjordan June 1918

153   On the plain in Jordan

155 Remains of a tomb in Judaean Hills

156 Crusaders castle Transjordan 1918

154 Northern banks of the Dead Sea Transjordan Valley

152   Judaean foothills at sundown

135 The Dead Sea looking Eastwards

133 Mountains of Moab to North of Dead Sea

134 Mountains of Moab at northern end of the Dead Sea.

131 Cherith brook where it flows into the river Jordan

132   The Dead Sea from the North 1918

144   el Arish December1916

165   Wadi el Arish from camp

002   Brigade HQ at Marakeb   May 1917

Headquarters at Marakeb

166   **Wadi el Arish in flood Dec. 1916**

146   **Sand dunes at el Burj Dec.1916**

140   **Looking across the plain at el Arish. Dec 1916.**

139   Sheikh's tomb at el Arish

143   Panorama at el Arish

142   Barren landscape el Arish Dec 1916

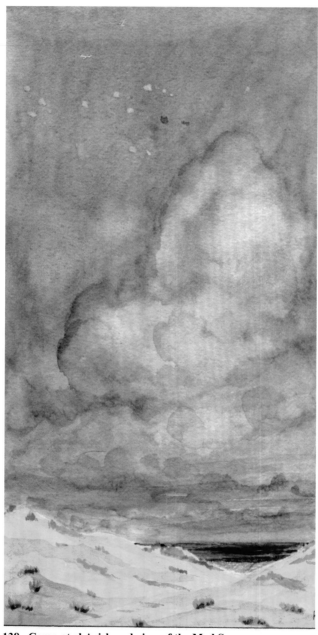

138   Camp at el Arish and view of the Med.Sea.

141   Clouds above the sea at el Arish

136   Washday at el Arish camp Judaea 1916

001 shelling Cape Helles 1915

137 El Arish Judaea

This is a small image of the wonderful painting by Lady Butler of the combined Cavalry charge at Huj made bymembers of the Worcestershire and Warwickshire Yeomanry. Twelve field guns were captured and ten machine guns. The enemy was routed and the infantry took 2000 prisoners.

APPENDIX 2

Photographs taken from the collection of Maj. Paul Fowler-Smith of equipment used by the Regiment in WW1. With acknowledgement.(Copyright reserved by owner)

*Tobacco tin and contents Christmas 1914 given to all Volunteers
by Queen Alexandra*

**Riding crop given by Lord Dudley Colonel of the Regiment to
all serving members of the Q.O.W.H.1914.**

Light desert uniform issued to Q.O.W.H 1915.
Topee with veil.(Never used without regimental orders)
Bandolier 50 rounds,Gauntlets for the R.S.M.

Maxim's Machine Gun, Produced in 1884 by Sir Hiram Maxim This was the gun used in Gallipoli by the Yeomanry.Soon after it was superceded by the Hotchkiss M.G.

APPENDIX 3
GALLIPOLI POST MORTEM

the British artillery on the open slopes. But they managed to win back their los
trenches, and by midday on August 10 not a single height of any importance a
Suvla or Anzac was in British hands. At Cape Helles the battle subsided to a
fitful end.

It was apparent only that the Allies had been incomparably the losers. During
the 259 days that elapsed between the first landings in April 1915 and the
final withdrawal in January 1916 they sent half a million men to Gallipoli, and
slightly more than half of these became casualties. There is some doubt abou
the exact number of the Turkish losses, but they are officially computed a
251,000, which is just one thousand less than those suffered by the. Allies; and
this perhaps is the best indication of how closely the struggle was fought.

The offical figures were: ALLIES Soldiers engaged: British: 410.000, French: 79.000 - 489.00(
Casualties: British: 205.000, French: 47.000 - 252.000
TURKS Soldiers engaged: Approximately: 500.000 Casualties: Killed: 55.127,
Wounded: 100.177, Missing: 10.067, Died of disease: 21.498, Evacuated sick: 64.440 - 251.30£

Lone Pine Cemetery and Memorial Gallipoli

APPENDIX 4

Suvla Bay

by W. H. Littlejohn

Old rose and black and indigo, Saffron streaks in a spume-tipped grey, Purple, laved in the dawn's wan glow - God, how fair you are, Suvla Bay! Spitting shrapnel and shrieking steel, brave men dead in their youth's noonday, all the anguish their loved ones feel is your Ambrose, fair Suvla Bay!

Stabbing sun from a brazen sky, Choking dust from the corpse-strewn way, each one treads as he marches by, - God, how I loathe you, Suvla Bay!Tanned men delving with labored breath, Stinking lighters discharging hay, Grey-hulled battleships belching death, God, there's work on at Suvla Bay!Pale, pale moon and the cold North Star, You who watch while I kneel and pray, take to her in the northland far one sobbing prayer from Suvla Bay!One sobbing prayer that the dull heart-pain God in heaven Thou alone canst stay, for her be stilled till I come again Back to her side from Suvla Bay!

Gallipoli

EPILOGUE TO GALLIPOLI
Taken from Lord Cobham's account, in the Regimental History of Q.O.W.H. 1914- 1922.

On October 31st 1915 the Regiment embarked on lighters at "C" beach under Lali Baba to transship into the Ermine, a small troop carrier plying between and the Gallipoli beaches. The hawsers between the lighters and the troopship broke in the rough sea drifting away with most of the men still aboard.
They approached again butting into the Ermine with their noses or tails butting against the ship until everyone was aboard. There they stayed for the night until daybreak. They were glad to see the last

of the famous peninsula, destined to rank for all time among those proud monuments the heroism of the British soldier. The story is one of a long-drawn-out bitter struggle

Struggle between opponents who fought each other all day with rifle and bomb, and at night crept out and stabbed each other in the dark. There was no release from the strain of watching and listening and sudden death. In common with the Turk, who in the main was a brave and chivalrous opponent and an extraordinarily stubborn fighter, the invaders had to contend with enemies far more insidious and debasing, in the shape of dirt and disease, lack of water, monotonous food and the plague of flies.

In August there were practically none, in September and October there were myriads. In the trenches there was no shade; sanitary arrangements were less than primitive, scraps of meat, half-emptied jam tins, sugar and other refuse lay everywhere in the dust and every man had his small store of food nearby. There were often the dead bodies of men and the remains of mule carcasses exposed to the sweltering heat and everywhere accessible to the foul swarms.

The tired troops, after the disturbance of the nights, tried to sleep through the hot afternoons in the trenches, but there were few who could enjoy that luxury. Some indeed from sheer exhaustion lay still for a time, with the flies crawling on their faces, crowding round their eyes and crawling unmolested about their open mouths; but to the larger number, the torment was beyond endurance, and the much needed repose denied.

All the survivors will carry to their graves the memories of those long months of bitter struggles and incredible hardships, of blood-soaked ground won by inches from the slopes of encircling hills, and of that strange sweet, musty smell, the smell of the Peninsula, which no man can ever forget.

APPENDIX 5

Q.O.W.H
by Oscar Teichmann
A Cambridge Graduate (Cornville & Caius College)
M.A.,M.B.,B. Chir.   (for private circulation only)

Nineteen fourteen, fourth of August did our unit mobilise, And six months were spent in guarding the East Coast against surprise.
The "Eloby" and "Saturnia" took our yeomen overseas,
After crossing Bay of Biscay they were more or less at ease.
At dusty, fly blown Chatby, in Alexandria's Bay,
Worcester Yeomen, jaundiced yellow, waited for the promised day.
In that scorp-infested district, the Bay of Aboukir,
Worcester Yeoman, now impatient, hoped 'der tag' was drawing near
At length the' "Ascania" bore them to the roads of Mudros Bay,
Hostile submarines to baffle, her course zigzagged all the way.
Near the hills of Anafarta, on the sands of Suvla Bay,
Queen's Own Yeomanry of Worcester shared the honours of the day.

On Chocolate Hill and Salt Lake, many a gallant Yeoman fell,
By machine gun, shrapnel, rifle fire, and high explosive shell.
For months our yeomen helped to keep the Osmanlis at bay,
Until a transport took them off and sailed West, Mudros way.
On board the ancient "Hannibal" once ship of some renown,
The Yeomen stoked and brought her safe to Alexandria town.
Under blazing sun of Mena, many centuries looked down,
From the Pyramids of Gizeh, on our Yeomen sunburnt brown.
Katia and Oghratina found the Worcesters staunch and true,
They fought and died and would not leave the RE in the blue.

After battle of Romani was the great advance begun,
And our Yeomen plodding deeply kept the enemy on the run.
Meanwhile the Desert Railway was advancing day by day,
As the natives filled their sand baskets and chanted Ho-Ha-Ray.
Near the mountain of Ruisat, where across the desert sands,
El Maghara rises sombre, the lone Hod, El Bayud stands.
Here the Worcesters held an outpost long way distant from rail-head,
Far removed from tiresome Generals and Brass Hats gold and red.
Beauteous Hod of mighty palm trees, silhouetted 'gainst the skies
Endless vista of the desert, amidst golden sand hills lies
Tho' thy water may be brackish, sand engulf thee tree by tree,
Thy great loneliness and beauty will for all time enthral me.
On the summit of the sand ridge and far from the madding crowd,
So impressed by awful grandeur, one is loth to speak aloud!
And o'er this wide flung desert Lilliputian man contests,
For supremacy by battle, as aforetime, East 'gainst West.
In the valley 'neath the palm trees, bleached white by Eastern sun,
Are the bones of Turkish soldiers, who have long the great race run.
When night falls on Hod El Bayud doth the desert stillness reign,
Spectres of the Moslem heroes hover o'er the ground again.
But now the march continues, horses plodding thro' the sand,
Route of Moses and Napoleon leading to the Promised Land.

At El Arish, ancient fortress, Egypt's river meets the sea,
After victory at Rafah, Asia's frontier stones we see.

Next, tragedy of Gaza, for we thought the battle won,
When orders to retire were given although' the Turk was done.
At battle of Two Gaza fell many a Yeoman bold?

But then at last the facts leaked out and so the truth was told.
A new C in C commands us and confidence inspires,
By giving many "Bowler Hats" which everyone admires?
One day the Chief came driving along the outpost line
In an old Ford car with one SO instead of eight or nine.

One Yeoman said to another, "And who's that bloke with him?"

"That's Lincoln Bennett's agent, with bowlers broad of brim!"

And the refrain of the Yeomen as they on their horses sat,
Was that disrespectful ditty of the modest bowler hat.

"There's a little black bowler for Tommy,
And a little grey bowler for John;
The one that is higher,
We're keeping for F-er
The other old T-lor's got on"
"There's a permanent bowler for Peter,
And a temporary one for D-bell;
One made in a hurry
For Arch---ld Murr---y,
And one for Belinda as well"

For the Wade of El Guzzhe where across the broad barley lands,
Lies the well known ridge El Buggar, the lone camp of Gamli stands.
To the north is Tel El Fara, in the south in Goz Mabruk,
Eastward lies the Goz El Basal, westward, Shauth and Harifuk
Here our Yeomen fought and shivered on the chilly outpost line,
Always keeping touch with Fara, three am to half past nine
'Til the advance on Beersheba, thirty five miles in a night,
Then the affair of Ras El Naga, a very bloody fight.
But the Worcesters and the Warwicks their greatest laurels won, When two hundred gallop'd the guns at Huj, sabring Turk and Hun.
Twelve guns and four machine guns they captured on that day,
Making a way for the 60th Division led by Shea.
Suvla, Katia and Romani, Huj, Salt, Rafah and Ballin,
Joined the Yeomanry of Worcester in the roar of battle's din
Also Gaza and Beersheba, Ras El Nag and Jericho,
Nebi Samwil and Damascus, El Nablus and Megiddo.

Gallant Queen's Hussars of Worcester, best of fellows staunch and true,
May the memory ever flourish of the men who fell for you.

For many a valiant Yeoman lies resting in the East,
Whose name we pledge in silence at this our Annual Feast.

Relieving Guard
By: Bret Harte
In memory of a friend, 1864
"No sight, no sound?" "No, nothing save
The plover from the marshes calling
On Came the Relief. "What Sentry, ho!
How passed the night through thy long waking?"
"Cold, cheerless, dark – as may befit
The hour before the dawn is breaking."
in yon western sky, about
An hour ago, a star was falling."
"A Star? There's nothing strange in that."
"No, nothing; but above the thicket,
Somehow it seemed to me that God
Somewhere had just relieved a picket."

2. Extracts; Yeomanry Cavalry of Worcestershire 1914 - 1922

Owing to the withdrawal of several Yeomanry Regiments for service in France, considerable reorganisation had been taking place, and the 5th Mounted Brigade was broken up. It was sad to say goodbye to the Warwickshire Yeomanry with still much to be done. Suvla Bay, Romani, Rafa and Gaza, and the bloody brotherhood of Huj provide an unbreakable chain to bind together the Yeomanry regiments of the two most beautiful counties of the English midlands.

The troopship carrying Yeomanry forces to the western front at the time of the final German advance in France with Major Grey Cheape on board was disastrously sunk off Alexandria by a German e-boat with considerable loss of life for men and horses – mostly Warwickshire Yeomen (27th May 1918).

The Regiment ceased to exist as cavalry on 31st March 1922 but distinguished itself again in the retreat to Dunkirk in 1940 and in the airborne landings in Normandy on D-Day 1943.

The railway line north of Semakh at the southern end of the Sea of Galilee had been wrecked, its tunnels blown up and bridges destroyed. All supplies from the rapidly moving Desert Mounted Corps had to be transported between Nazareth and Damascus by motor Lorries. In the face of diminishing opposition, Damascus fell to British cavalry assisted by the troops of the Hedjaz commanded by Colonel Lawrence (of Arabia). The Regiment descended from the Judaean highlands to the plain of Esdrailon through the pass of Megiddo (Armageddon) to Afule, Nazareth & Beisan with Mount Carmel rearing its blue mass to the north-east and the Jordan valley on the right. Nazareth shone white on the hills ahead.

The camp at El Afule – a station on the Haifa to Damascus railway, was full of mosquitoes, which interfered with sleep. This place was undoubtedly responsible for the outbreak of malaria which devastated the regiment during the next three months; 20 Warwickshire Yeomen died of this and of infective hepatitis at Damascus.

Near the road to Galilee lay the town of Tiberius, encircled by its old Roman walls. Owing to the presence of cholera, the regiment was not allowed to enter it nor bathe in the river. Nazareth had been the HQ of the German General, Lyman Von Sanders, and the 13th Cavalry Brigade (Gloucestershire Yeomanry) entered the town from the south while the General escaped in his staff car from the north. Allenby was not pleased.

Few of the regiment had opportunities of seeing anything of the beautiful city of Damascus but its squalid side, and remember it chiefly by the discomfiture of its hospitals, and the leisure with which they finally steamed away on the rickety railway to Beirut and a hospital ship.

River Barada in Damascus
The remaining fit members marched back to Judd, with a large number of horses being ridden by Turks and Germans and the consequent long journey to Cairo. It is difficult to determine whether all these horses were taken to Cairo for disposal.

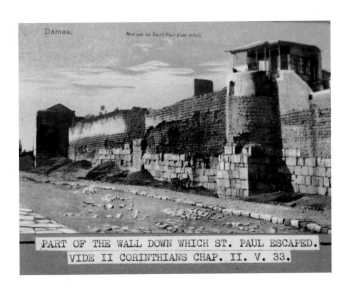

PART OF THE WALL DOWN WHICH ST. PAUL ESCAPED.
VIDE II CORINTHIANS CHAP. II. V. 33.

42 French troops enter Damascus, deposing King Feisal and
bringing an end to Syria's brief independence, 1920

3. Demobilisation

*Shall we never again ride knee to knee in the pomp of the
squadron line,*
*with headropes white as a mountain drift and curb chains all
ashine?*
*Will they dawn no more those glorious days when the world
seemed all our own,*
Who rode as scouts on an errant quest, alive, alert and alone?
(WKH)

The Regiment, with its horses, arrived in Cairo from Damascus on
4th December 1918. During the time spent in camp, several men
died of influenza which swept Europe after the war, and instead of
returning home to England the regiment was deployed in Jaffa to
maintain law and order in Palestine after the absence of Ottoman
and any German officials.

By May 1919 the numbers were down to 15 officers, 167 other
ranks and 171 horses. Fortunately they were not aboard the ship
which was torpedoed on its way to France. In July the remaining
men and horses were embarked at Port Said under the command of
Captain Haynes-Rudge who served with the regiment from Sept
1914, including the six months at Gallipoli.

On arrival in Worcester they were paraded before the Lord
Lieutenant (the Earl of Coventry), Lieutenant Colonel Coventry,
the Mayor and the Corporation to great acclaim. They had
suffered the greatest losses of all the cavalry regiments on the
Palestinian front.

4. Extracts from service personnel at Gallipoli.

Marine Joe Clement: Royal Marine Light Infantry tells of the quiet evacuation from Gallipoli January 1916.

There was continuous rain which filled up the trenches, so we had to sleep on the parapets. The Turks did the same. We had an unspoken truce and didn't shoot at sleeping men. But it was so cold and we were always wet. On Christmas Day we were in the firing line and were served one slice of pudding and seven dates. Two days later we went down into our dug-out to change our clothes only to find our packs with our clean washing under three feet of water. Then, for another treat, they put us into the firing line for New Year's Day.

The first we knew of the evacuation was when the French moved out on the 1st January. We spread out into their trenches to extend the line. We didn't know that Anzac and Suvla beaches had already been evacuated. On the 8th of January we began to destroy food and rifles that were not needed. We then tied empty sandbags around our feet, secured our water bottles so that they wouldn't clank around, and at midnight we moved off. I carried my machine gun over five miles in the dark until we reached the beach. As we were walking 'Asiatic Annie' fired several shells. We had come to hate her throughout our time at Gallipoli. The Turks didn't know we were going. Firing from the Asiatic side, Annie had always been a law unto herself.

We landed on Suvla beach and all that first day we were lying there with no orders to attack. Throughout the day the Turks were reinforcing their positions. I kept in touch with my Colonel – I had to be close to him because I was one of the chief runners who took down messages, but by the time we had reached Point 100, which was our objective, our casualties had mounted terrifically. The Colonel turned to me and said, 'You must go down and find the Brigadier.' It was a verbal message, there was no time for writing it down or anything. The message was, 'Have reached Point 100. Casualties very heavy, am being enfiladed.'

I show off downhill with this message. On the way I was hit on the top of the head with a nose-cap from a shell, which crushed my helmet and slightly wounded me on the side. I think there was more blood than damage but I didn't look a very good sight by the time I reached the Brigadier General. I explained the position to him and he looked at me as much as to say, 'We haven't been in action two or three hours yet, it was impossible.' But a few minutes later a Lincolnshire runner came up and he had the same tale, their casualties were about seventy-five per cent. I remember the General looking at the Brigade Major and said, 'My God, this must be true.'

Ordinary Seaman Jack Gearing: Benbow Battalion, Royal Naval Division tells of the Suvla bay Landing
We knew that the four

hundred men of the East Yorks were mostly fresh from training and few had seen action, so every sailor was given two soldiers to look after. We gave them our hammocks, made sure they ate well and gave them our run. You see, we knew that where they were going would be like Hell on earth, so we gave them all the love we could, because they were going to need it. There was all those feelings, all that silence. That's why I admire the British, they take it and they're quiet.

As we approached Suvla Bay on the night of 6/7 August, it was the darkness before the dawn. I stood on the gangway which had been fitted over the stem to allow the troops to walk down into the motor lighters. As the soldiers followed each other down with their rifles, one got hit by a sniper and screamed out. I told him to shut up and put up with the pain or he would frighten the rest – that was my first scream of war.

APPENDIX 6

Copy of a letter to Victor Godrich from Jack Middleton dated the 3rd May 1916

The Battle of KATIA and OGRATINA took place on Sunday 23rd April 1916

Dear Vic,

You may have heard that we had a rotten smash up on Easter Sunday and I am very sorry to tell you that poor old Cyril was killed. Bousfield and Hugh Field are among the missing. I am very much afraid that they were both killed. In fact there were only 5 that got away out of the Gun Section – the only man you would remember was Alf Daw.

I was darned lucky to be out of it, I was down at Ismalia going through a Gun Course at a special Instructors School there under Major Charteris. I managed to get a 1st Class Instructor's Certificate. Poor old Worcester Yeomanry, my God they did go through it! The Turks have got some prisoners but how many we cannot tell as they stripped all the dead even to identity discs and as they were buried by a Relief Force of Australians no-one knows who was killed or captured.

Our casualties amounted to at least 150 (take the first three figures of my number and add about 40 and you will have got it) so you may guess what a plight we are in.

*I cannot tell you where it was as you know **this letter will be censored and might not get through**.*

I have written to Cyril's Uncle, to Bousfield's people and to George Field – have told the latter two that they are missing (only) so be careful what you say if you meet them.

Poor old Cyril was identified by some means or other and was buried with some of the other lads.

Kemp and Shortie are in England on leave and I am the only one of the Gun Section boys left who were on the Peninsula, so you can guess my feelings.

*A and D Squadrons **lost all**, C Squadron lost 63. What they are going to do with us is unknown at the present. We are certainly useless as we are.*

I took the liberty (which I hope you will forgive) of opening your letter to Cyril, also some of Bousfield's and Hugh Field's and I have burnt them all. I hardly knew what to do but thought this was best.

Well old man, I wish I was back In old Blighty once more, if only for a rest. I can imagine what a time you boys will be having and how shocked you will be to hear the news.

I hope old man that you will have recovered from the rotten fever. I believe it was dysentery you had, and feel no ill effects.

I am pleased to say I am much better and feel very little of the effects of the frostbite.

Give my kindest regards to any of the boys you may meet.

Your old chum, (sgd) Jack Middleton.

Explanatory notes :

- Full strength of Machine Gun Section was 20 men. About half the strength were evacuated from Gallipoli in 1915 with stomach trouble
- Cyril Combs was my own particular friend, he was promoted Corporal in my place when I was evacuated
- Casualties quoted in letters were not allowed. Unfortunately no-one knows the right number
- C Squadron casualties, smaller than A or D, due to the fact that they were not at Katia or Ogratina when the battle started .Frost bite on Gallipoli – 200 casualties

2nd Lieut.Anthony Ffrench Blake newly Commissioned.

APPENDIX 7

Extracts from Major Ffrench Blake's Diary (8th July 1916 – 19TH APRIL 1917) kept in Worcs Yeo.Museum Trust.

   1.   Battle of Rafa

Mounted Brigade to be in BITTIA by 6.00 am preceding the Infantry of 52nd Division.

Moved to BITTIA 2.30 am Worcs HQ Glos Warwicks

2 camel Corps sent to GAZA

23 Dec 1916 Wilson & Albright made Captains
Battle of Magdaba – news scanty, but apparently ALH(Australian Light Horse) Division surrounded the Turks and got some prisoners. Description follows.
Officers killed 5, wounded 7, OR dead 17, wounded 117, Horses dead 27, wounded 32, 1377 prisoners taken, 4 guns, 6 boxes ammo, 100,000 rounds SAA, 3 Krupps guns from EL ARISH fort in WADI.
Rained heavily in night – a verv meagre Xmas!

25 Dec 1916 Rode over to Bir MASHI to see David Finlay (7DG) Bde Major NZMR. Had excellent lunch with General Chaytor who told me all about the battle, then Finlay came back and I saw him for a bit.
To O/C A Squadron
Special Order of the Day by Brigadier General E A Wiggin

11th Jan 1917 I cannot find words to adequately express my pleasure and gratification at the splendid behaviour of the 5th Mounted Brigade together with 'B' Battery HAC in the recent victory at RAFA. The Brigade were called upon to perform an exceedingly difficult task, made more so by the wonderful defensive position the enemy had taken up, and one and all acquitted themselves in the manner I always knew they would so should the occasion present itself. It proved beyond all doubt that the energy and enthusiasm with which Officers and all ranks tackled the severe training which at times has been asked of them, had borne its fruit in due season and I can only offer you my most sincere thanks for the loyalty and devotion the Brigade displayed on this their day of trial.
Before concluding, there are two subjects which touch me and I know we all feel the same, that is the regret and sorrow we feel for our fallen and wounded comrades, and again we must congratulate our brothers in Arms, the Anzac Mounted Division and the Camel Corps on their wonderful zeal and prowess with which they came over the top. E A Wiggin, Brigadier General Commanding 5th Mounted Brigade

2nd Extract from Ffrench Blake Diary (GAZA 1917)
Last signal (2nd Battle of Gaza) to OC Worcs Yeomanry : 19th April 1917

0925 I am in a small tributary wadi at foot of ridge we have just crossed. *He was leading an advance into strongly held Turkish positions.The advance of the Gloucesters up the other side of the wadi failed,so he was pinned down and fatally shot in the head .He was a very keen efficient and brave officer.*

17ᵗʰ April 1917: news of the day
Austria asks for separate peace
Germany admits internal troubles
France attacks on 40 mile front and takes 10,000 prisoners
British get Loos in France – 14,000 prisoners and 96 guns
75ᵗʰ Division arriving in Egypt
But the war went on until 11 November 1918.
19ᵗʰ April 1917: the Regiment was shelled heavily from 7.20 am until 6.30 pm. By 11.00 am the QOWH were under the Atweina redoubt in close contact with the Turkish fortifications.

APPENDIX 8
Photographs taken during 1914 -1918
Four Old Boys from K.E.G.S. Birmingham

Lean and hungry in the desert at Gaza 1917.E.V.G. has his wrists in bandages on a/c desert sores and fragile skin.(Vitamin def)

Territorial Camping pre-War

234

E.V.G.carving the joint at el Fara .100 C.This is where he got sunstroke due to lack ofcover

Taking horses to water down the Wadi Ghuzzi

Convalescent at Malvern.April 1916 A snow blizzard was the cause of the leaning telephone post.

Naked centaurs bathing in the Med at el Arish

Figtree saddle rack el Arish rest camp by the sea.E.V.G. wears puttees.

The solo card playing four. Whalley Hospital1915

E.V.G. back at work with the Post Office.1919

Split-up ahead

THE Anglican Archbishop in Jerusalem, the 'Most Rev. George Appleton, who is retiring at 71, looks like being the last Anglican Archbishop to reside in the Holy City.

There will, I understand, be no successor to him. The vast area of the archepiscopate, which includes North Africa, is likely to be divided into separate bishoprics.

Founded some 15 years ago, the Jerusalem Archbishopric has provided

Bowing out

an Anglican presence through the troubled years of the Arab-Israeli conflict. But it has involved considerable feats of diplomacy.

With Anglican congregations mostly Arab in their sympathies, Archbishop Appleton's intimate knowledge of Jewry has been an asset to his influence. His success is reflected by the fact that his privately-circulated news-letter, *Ends and Odds*, has been sought eagerly by both Jews and Arabs.

5.9.73

The Anglican Archbishop of Jerusalem who confirmed E.V.G to the Protestant Faith 1916.

MUSTAFA KEMAL

Kemal Ataturk, who led the Turkish forces to repel the Suvla Bay landing.He was promoted to Colonel on the spot and took command of their forces on the peninsula from his stone hut. He went on to depose the Caliphate and became leader of the modern state of Turkey. Gallipoli has become a sacred place for all the Turks who visit their national monument in Thousands.

On leave Port Said August 1917.

241

Panorama picture of Dardanelles

Anzac Beach Gallipoli, Officers coming!

Allied fleet busy bombarding entrance to Dardanelles

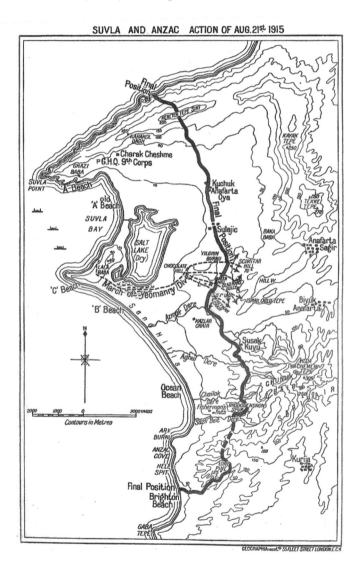

SUVLA AND ANZAC ACTION OF AUG. 21st 1915

243

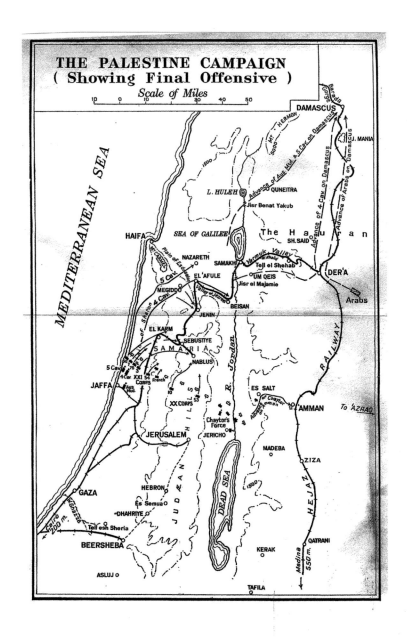